Monarch Illustrated Guide to

BASIC CAR CARE

by A. M. Pettis

Richard Balkin
Consulting Editor

MONARCH

THIS BOOK IS DEDICATED TO MY WIFE, FLORENCE, WHO EDITED AND TYPED THE MANUSCRIPT AND PROVIDED THE ENCOURAGEMENT AND INSPIRATION THAT MADE THIS BOOK POSSIBLE.

Acknowledgments

The author gratefully acknowledges the contributions of Gerald R. McKay, who took photographs and contributed to the manuscript; George Yates, who contributed information and served as technical adviser on American cars; and Rudolph Arndt, who made contributions and reviewed the information on foreign cars. Appreciation is expressed to Mary N. Harrison for data provided and suggestions on certain portions.

Suggestions and assistance came from George E. Agner, Larry O. Bagnall, L. B. Baldwin, Linda R. Baldwin, Curt Cannady, George E. Davis, Jr., Ken Dykhuis, Earl Ferrence, Emily King, Ted Orton, D. C. Pettis, D. M. Pettis, Mike Prater, Ed L. Wells, and Carlton L. Zink.

Contents

Shock absorbers
Additives

Introduction

Fifty-six million women and sixty-nine million men drive vehicles in the United States. This book is written primarily to help those men and women who want to look after their own cars. The information applies to many American cars and foreign cars. It is essential in this modern age that a driver know some of the component parts of the car and have an understanding of normal maintenance and service procedures. This book is not designed to make a mechanic of anyone. Technical manuals are available for practically all cars. To be a competent mechanic requires special schooling and training on the job under the guidance of an experienced supervisor.

If your community has a reliable, knowledgeable, honest automobile mechanic, treat him royally. Bake or buy him a cake when an occasion arises—such as his birthday, Christmas, or the Fourth of July. He is a skilled craftsman whose advice, opinion, and assistance will help you over many a rough spot. To find a desirable mechanic with the traits I have listed may not be easy. Talk with friends and acquaintances who have lived in the community for several years. Of course, if your car needs repairs while under warranty, take the car to the dealer who sells that make.

Owning or driving a car ceased to be a luxury in this country more than a generation ago, so there is no need to dwell on our dependence on the automobile. Even energy shortages and high costs have not convinced many drivers to forego their own vehicles for public transportation for most trips. Each one of us wants to go when and where he pleases. Public transportation may not offer a choice to fill our needs, and even when it does, we often prefer our own conveyances. Self-service filling stations are becoming quite popular in many areas of the country. By pumping the gas yourself you can save money, but it is up to you to clean the windshield and check under the hood.

Here we go then on a compact reference to help drivers know what is under the hood and what to do when that "Blivet Eight" or "Super Six" or "Economy Four" refuses to go or acts up in disconcerting ways. One of my sons is an excellent amateur auto mechanic, but on the other hand my wife and daughter and another son care nothing about what is under the hood. An automobile ignition key is to them a magic carpet that takes them from point A to point B. They do, of course, realize that every so often a stop at a service station is necessary for gas, tune-ups, and repairs, but truthfully their interest in car care goes little beyond that point. But now it is practical and popular for men and women to know more about this creature that has become entwined in their lives; the rising cost of maintenance has made this a virtual necessity.

Vehicles are usually the most expensive investments that families make other than their home. I cannot overemphasize the importance of preventive maintenance and proper service of your car. This will not only save you money but also will make the difference between having an economical car or one that is continually breaking down and requiring expensive repairs.

All parts wear out sooner or later; this includes brake linings, spark plugs, and shock absorbers, to name just a few. Do not think you are just unlucky or that you have failed in preventive maintenance when certain parts have to be replaced. However, if you take care of a car, it will look after you more than 99 44/100 percent of the time, which is better than the purity of Ivory soap. But if you fail to have the car serviced at regular intervals, either in your own or in a mechanic's garage, it will surely repay you by breaking down and giving you expensive repair bills. A car that is not properly maintained is an unsafe vehicle, endangering the lives of you—the driver—and others in and out of the car.

OWNER'S MANUAL

To begin the learning process, locate the booklet found in most glove compartments, called the Owner's Manual. It may contain unfamiliar words and terms, but this book can save you money.

Service procedures vary between different makes of cars and between the newer cars and those manufactured several years ago, so follow the service recommendations given in your Owner's Manual. It will tell you when to change the engine oil and the oil filter, when to grease the car, when to service the air cleaner, and when to repack the front wheel bearings. Remember that a new car warranty requires that service work be done as the manual recommends in order to keep the warranty in effect.

INSTRUMENT PANEL

The instrument panel is the headquarters office of an automobile. Each make of car and each year's model have slightly different instrument panels, but basically all are alike. They have instruments—dials, gauges, "idiot lights"—that give you, the driver, a message. Most experienced drivers hate the idiot lights and feel manufacturers should go back to providing gauges for most information. For example, when the red light on the temperature indicator (TEMP) appears, the engine is already overheated and may even be damaged. With a pointer-type heat indicator, you have advance warning and can act accordingly. If the oil pressure light (OIL) comes on while your car is moving, something is wrong; perhaps the oil pressure is low, which may cause severe damage to the engine. Other red lights on the instrument panel indicate that the alternator (GEN) is not producing electricity, that your emergency brake (BRAKE) is on, or (along with a buzzer) that your seat belts are not fastened. If any red light appears while you are driving, pull over to the side of the road and stop. Then turn to the pertinent sections of this book to help decide your next move.

The fuel gauge (FUEL) obviously tells you the amount of fuel in your tank. Some gasoline gauges are accurate, some are not. Most gauges purposely indicate "E" (empty) while you still have at least one gallon. To be on the safe side, have your tank filled when the gauge reads empty and compare the number of gallons needed to fill the tank with the number of gallons that the tank holds, as shown in the Owner's Manual; the difference will tell you how many gallons you actually have left when the gauge reads empty.

The speedometer indicates the speed in miles per hour; some newer cars also may have small numbers indicating kilometers per hour (see the chart comparing miles and kilometers in Chapter 21, Preventive Maintenance Schedule Summary). Under the speedometer is the odometer, which registers miles traveled. Located near the speedometer are the turn signal light pointers. These flash at the same time as the turn signal lights on the outside of the car. The turn signal lever is usually found on the steering column, and it activates the turn signal lights.

Many controls vary with makes and years of cars. Refer to your Owner's Manual for the location and operation of light switches, gearshift selector, windshield wiper-washer control, and others.

THINGS TO REMEMBER

The mere mention of record-keeping will stop some of you at this point. If you do not want to keep records showing when things were done, then how will you know that it is time to take your car to have service work done or to do it yourself? A car costs too much money for you to *guess* about when it is time for service. I am not that good a guesser. The only way I can know *what* was done to my car and *when* is to write it down. So there we have it! There is no other way to take care of your car properly than to write down all the facts as they happen and do things as needed.

Use the service schedule pamphlet, if your car has one. Some people prefer to keep a notebook in the glove compartment. I keep a small notebook on the visor of my car for recording the gallons of gasoline put in the tank and the mileage, so at any time I can calculate the miles per gallon I am getting. Some service stations write routine servicing on a gummed label and place it on the lock wall of the driver's door. At home I keep a manila folder with receipts for all repair work done and for purchases such as tires, batteries, mufflers, and tailpipes. On the cover of the manila folder are facts concerning the mileage when all major service work was done, when the tires were rotated, when the front wheels were aligned, when the tailpipe, muffler, and radiator hoses were replaced, the date the battery was purchased, and so forth.

How and where you keep the information is not important. What really matters is that you agree with me that keeping information is absolutely necessary and that you start now to keep records on your car.

1

Buying a Car

You probably have more money invested in an automobile than in any other asset besides your home. Since you may buy and sell many cars during your lifetime, careful shopping and the right choice will not only save you a lot of money but will spare you many of the headaches acquired by impulsive car buyers.

SIZE AND FEATURES

What size car meets your requirements? Consider a smaller car than you would like to have, because it will probably give better gas mileage. (Fuel prices are expected to go even higher than they are.) Comfortable seating space is one requirement if your family travels together. Adequate storage space may be important. If you are in a car pool, you may need a car larger than a compact. A full-sized car will be more comfortable and safer than a compact for extensive traveling on the highway. A station wagon may be the best choice for the family that travels with small children or goes tent camping. A pickup truck has advantages for the family that hauls materials, and it can be used with a pickup camper.

AMERICAN OR FOREIGN CARS

Should you buy an American car or a foreign car? There are strong opinions on both sides. Since most foreign governments tax cars on the basis of the size of the engine, and since fuel prices are higher in most foreign countries than in the United States, foreign car manufacturers and their engineers have devoted more of their efforts than have

American manufacturers to developing smaller cars with more efficient engines. Most foreign cars get exceptionally good gas mileage, a feature that now attracts American buyers. Since the early fifties, several makes of foreign cars have become quite common in this country.

Take the time to consider your needs before you buy a foreign car, especially if it is to be the only car in your household. The inconvenience, delay, and expense of repairing and servicing a foreign car may be frustrating and costly, particularly if you do much long-distance driving. Volkswagen has done one of the best jobs of any foreign car manufacturer in establishing dealerships and parts sources in most areas of the United States. On the other hand, a foreign make that is not very popular and does not have many dealers and parts sources can give you almost insurmountable problems if the car breaks down on a trip.

Even if you only use your foreign car locally, you will want to be certain that the dealer you bought it from stocks parts for the car and has a mechanic trained to repair that make and model. I know someone who bought a foreign car from a dealer who also sold a well-known American make in a city with a population of about 100,000. When the car broke down, my friend had to take the car about a hundred miles to a larger city in order to get the needed repairs.

New- and used-car dealers are aware of the difficulty of getting parts and service for certain foreign cars and they may offer you far less than you expect when you try to trade in or sell one. On the other hand, certain foreign makes, such as Mercedes-Benz and Volkswagen, hold their value well; the little-known, unpopular foreign cars tend to depreciate more rapidly.

ACCESSORIES

Choose accessories carefully. Automatic transmission is easier to drive, but it costs more to operate than a manual shift; fuel consumption is higher, and the transmission service and repair is more frequent. Power steering and power brakes may help the senior citizen whose reflexes have slowed or the man or woman who does not have much strength; but here, too, service and repair are more frequent.

Many other accessories are available for your consideration. Some are merely cosmetic, others make sense depending on where you live and what your needs are. Tinted glass will reduce the amount of heat in a car and is recommended if you buy air conditioning. The list of accessories available for most cars is endless, so do not make decisions impulsively in a showroom. Take the list home and scrutinize it carefully at your leisure. Free from a salesman's pressure, you will make more rational and less costly choices.

TRADE-INS

If you are like most new-car buyers, you'll be trading in a used car and you'll want the best price you can get. What can you do to make sure your car brings the top dollar? The appearance of the car is important, but a dealer or private party will not judge a book just by its cover. A fresh paint job looks good, but if it is hiding body damage it could hurt the sale, and a sloppy paint job definitely will. If your car needs repainting, a quality paint job in a professional shop should pay for itself by increasing the worth of the car. Keeping the car clean and waxed is the best protection against premature paint deterioration. The car should be cleaned and polished inside and out; clean the upholstery with shampoo and make the glass and metal surfaces spotless.

Engine condition is the next thing a potential buyer or appraiser is going to examine. The ease with which a car starts is extremely important, so invest in a tune-up or a new battery or whatever is necessary to achieve it; having the battery charged may be all that is needed.

Smart buyers usually want a mechanic to inspect a used car, and a car dealer definitely will have his mechanic look over your car. Before approaching a dealer, you might have your own mechanic check over your car and take care of defects, such as an obvious oil leak, that can kill a sale or lower the trade-in value. A gauge that is not operating or a burned-out light bulb will signal trouble in the buyer's mind and diminish the car's value. It may cost only a few dollars and take a small amount of your time to repair or replace such small items. The trade-in value can be increased by as much as $500 when a car is put in top shape. Incidentally, you will probably get more money for your car by selling it to a private party than by trading it in; an advertisement in the classified section of your local newspaper will bring interested callers.

NEW CARS

Do you really need a new car? Would a used car or a leased car do as well? Here are some factors that might convince you a new car is the best choice:

1. You have a car to trade in or a down payment that equals at least one-third or one-fourth of the total price.
2. Dependability in a car is extremely important to you.
3. You drive 1,000 miles a month or more.
4. You do extensive highway driving or drive miles away from home.
5. Status is important to you, and a new car means added prestige to you and your family.
6. You can afford a new car.
7. You do not mind spending money on style and are aware that a car depreciates most in its early life.

You can save money by buying "last year's model," one of the leftovers that are reduced in price when the new models are introduced around September or October. People usually have strong opinions about cars: manufacturer, size, type, features, color, etc. The more flexible you are the better your chances of finding more than one dealer who has a car that you would like to own. Shop and compare; you are likelier to get a good buy from a dealer who knows that you can get your needs met just as easily elsewhere.

You should not have to pay the sticker price on a new car. Buying a car is not like buying a suit of clothes or a dress; you should always be able to get a discount off the list price. Do not be afraid to bargain or to make the salesman a counteroffer.

Beware of misleading sales pitches. "Lowballing" refers to the practice of offering you a car at an extremely low price. When you go to other dealers to compare prices, you find that none of the others comes close. Upon returning to the first salesman to inform him you have decided to buy the car, he says that he will have to get the approval of the sales manager or the owner of the dealership. You are then informed that the price the salesman quoted was too low, and the company would lose money at that price; therefore, it will be necessary to add X number of dollars to the price. Since most customers are weary at this point and have their hearts set on that particular car, they go ahead and buy. I made the mistake of buying in a similar situation myself several years ago. I actually felt sympathetic toward the salesman because I thought he had made an honest mistake. Now I know the whole episode was planned, so I urge you to turn down a lowballing deal and buy from dealers who are more honest.

"Highballing" is another misleading sales gimmick. The dealer will quote a fantastic allowance for your old car, but he jacks up the new-car price either to list price or to a figure high enough to absorb the unusually high trade-in value he is giving you. Remember that the difference you have to pay is what counts.

"Dealer prep" is not a misleading gimmick, but a fair and honest charge on all new cars. It refers to the reimbursement to the dealer for the expense and time of preparing the car for delivery. It is an assurance to the buyer and the dealer that the car as sold is in mint condition.

When is a new car a good buy? Federal law requires manufacturers to post a sticker on the rear window of each new car quoting the manufacturer's suggested retail price, the accessories, and the transportation charges.

Here is a guideline to determine a fair price from a dealer: Subtract the transportation charges. Multiply the remaining figure by 85 percent for compacts, or by 80–83 percent for intermediates and full-size cars. To this sum, add back the transportation charges. This is the cost of the car to the dealer. To this figure add $150 to $300 for the dealer's operating costs, salesman's commission, and profit. This figure is approximately the lowest price for which a dealer will sell a car, no matter how much haggling is done.

Examine carefully the warranty or owner-service policy when you buy a new car. This is your written guarantee against defective parts and workmanship. Be certain you understand *what is* and *what is not* covered. Warranties are usually in effect for a period of time or mileage, whichever occurs first. To keep the warranty in effect, the owner must have servicing done at intervals recommended by the Owner's Manual. During the warranty period, it is important to have service work done by a reputable dealer or service station. Keep your receipts. You will need them if repairs are needed under warranty to prove you have fulfilled the servicing required.

If you are switching from a subcompact, a compact, or an intermediate to a full-size car (especially a luxury type), consider that the increased length or width of the car requires more room when parking. And do not forget the $64 question: will this superduper creampuff fit into your garage?

USED CARS

Most people who buy used cars do so because they cannot afford a new car of the type they want. Some people buy used cars for economical transportation, especially when the car is to be used only locally. The most expensive item a new-car owner faces is depreciation, which is greatest during the first year or two of a car's life. The new-car owner's loss can be your gain. You may decide that a used car is the best investment for your transportation needs if:

1. You do not travel extensively.
2. The car is a second car for the family.
3. The car will be transportation for a teen-ager.
4. You wish to spend only a limited amount of money.

Shop and compare when buying a used car. Generally you have two sources: a used-car dealer or a private owner. Read the ads in your local newspaper to locate used cars from both sources. If you have any doubts about a dealer's reputation, call the chamber of commerce or the Better Business Bureau. Reputable dealers expect to be in business a long time, and they are usually concerned about your satisfaction.

Dealers who have well-equipped service departments usually make the necessary repairs to put used cars in reasonably good condition before selling them, and they are more likely to offer warranties and to honor them. Dealers or used-car lots without service departments tend to sell cars "as they are." Franchised new-car dealers select the best of the cars traded in to sell on their used-car lots. The least desirable trade-ins are wholesaled to other used-car dealers.

Car salesmen earn their income from commissions on the cars they sell. Though some want to help you find the car that best fits your needs, most have little concern for your welfare and will not hesitate to pressure you to make a sale. Do not be hasty in buying an expensive item like a car. Be wary of "fantastic bargains" or warnings that another buyer has his eye on this "jewel" which is going to be snapped up unless you act at once.

Franchised dealers, banks, and other auto finance agencies keep a current "blue book" or N.A.D.A. book showing the wholesale and retail values of used cars. Once you locate a used car that you might want, find out from one of these sources the nationwide "average" wholesale and retail price of the car you have in mind, as equipped. This information is very helpful in haggling with a used-car salesman or in discussing a fair price with a private owner. A car with low mileage in superb condition is probably worth more than the "book value" listed in the current book, while a car with high mileage and showing wear and tear is worth less.

Make two checks before you close the deal on a used car. You, the buyer, should make the first check, and I am going to give you pointers to help you. If a car seems satisfactory and the price is right (or near enough so that you think you can get the seller to accept your lower offer), then you ought to have a mechanic check the car. He will charge you for this service, but the money is well spent because he may help you avoid buying a lemon and paying costly repair bills.

Do not buy the car if a dealer or private owner refuses to let you test-drive the car or take it to your mechanic. But do not automatically reject a car that has one or more things wrong with it. Find out the cost of putting the car in good operating condition and add this to the price; you may still be getting a good deal.

Your Check

Look over the outside of the car—the appearance can tell you a lot about how the previous owner has cared for the car and can also give you warning of trouble to come. Look for unmatching paint; the car was probably in an accident if a section has been repainted. A totally repainted car with paint on chrome moldings and rubber sealing strips may indicate that something had to be covered up. Another tip-off to major body repair is a fresh weld which shows up in the engine compartment, or trunk, or underneath the car. If the car is in a garage, take it outside where the light is better. Sight along the sides of the car to look for uneven places that may mean body work, a result of previous accidents. See that the doors, hood, and trunk open and close properly and fit well. If they do not, the problem could be a bent frame or body. If you or a mechanic conclude that the car has been in a major accident, turn it down at once.

Look for paint blisters, which usually result from rust. See if there is rust underneath the car, in the fender wells, in the trunk, and around the chrome strip on the back window. A car used near salt water, or on northern roads where salt is spread in winter, may show corrosion and damage to metal parts.

Examine the tread on all the tires for uneven wear. On front tires this may indicate a need for front-end alignment, worn front-end parts, or a bent frame caused by an accident. Uneven wear on the rear tires has a different meaning, depending on whether the car is American- or foreign-made. Uneven tire wear on the rear of an American car suggests —at the least—that the tire may need balancing or—at the worst—that there may be a major problem such as a bent frame from an accident. Tires wearing unevenly on the rear of a foreign car may indicate the rear wheels only need to be balanced, adjusted, or aligned. Of course, a bent frame may also cause this trouble. Foreign cars often have the rear wheels suspended independently, whereas American cars usually have a solid axle.

Rock the car by jumping on the bumper or pushing down hard at each corner. The car probably needs new shocks if it bounces more than twice after you let go.

Next look at the inside of the car. The interior sometimes gives a good indication about the car's use. A car with high mileage will have telltale signs, such as excessive wear on the floor mats or carpets. The driver's seat may be badly worn and sagging. The steering wheel of a high-mileage car may look worn, since after many miles the perspiration from the driver's hands can cause the finish to deteriorate. Look at the brake pedal, the clutch pedal (if the car has manual transmission), and the accelerator; unusual wear or a brand-new pedal indicates lots of driving.

You are ready for the road test if the car still looks promising. This might be a good time to drive the car to your mechanic and ask him to check it over. Your road test should include shifting gears, going over bumpy roads to test the shock absorbers, and steering around curves to see how much play is in the steering mechanism. The automatic transmission should not slip or hesitate as you shift from gear to gear. Any unusual noises in the transmission, especially when accelerating, may mean trouble. A car with manual transmission should shift smoothly and quietly through the gears. You have problems if the clutch slips or makes an unusual noise. Try the brakes: something is wrong if the car pulls to one side, the brakes feel spongy, or you hear strange noises when you push the brake pedal.

Your Mechanic's Check

An experienced mechanic can tell a great deal about the engine of a car just by starting it and listening to it run. He should also take a road test in the car. His trained eye can spot evidence of a major accident, excessive mileage, and trouble indicators that you might never notice. If you and your mechanic agree that more extensive testing is called for, he can check the engine compression, the brake linings, and various other components of the car to see if they need repairing or replacing.

A Final Precaution

During your check, you may notice apparently minor problems, such as a dashboard light that does not work or a turn signal that does not operate properly. Such a small repair may actually be expensive if the wiring to the dashboard or the entire turn signal mechanism has to be replaced. The safest procedure is to tell the used-car salesman that you will buy the car provided he will fix the item or items that malfunction and that you are willing to put up a deposit of $25 to show good faith. The seller should be glad to correct the trouble if the dash light only needs a new bulb; but if he is not, watch out!

Warranty

Ask for a warranty or guarantee in writing before you buy a used car from a dealer; the promises of a salesman are not binding. Warranties vary in content, so find out in detail exactly what is covered by the warranty and for how long, what is not covered, and who pays for labor. Some warranties given on used cars are on a fifty-fifty basis: you pay one-half and the dealer pays the other half of all repair costs for a certain time or mileage. Some warranties cover parts and labor, while others cover parts only. A used-car warranty may vary in length from thirty days to six months or longer. Many warranties require you to return the car to the seller for any repair work covered by the warranty.

At some franchised dealers, you can purchase an additional warranty on new and used cars. On new cars this warranty is in addition to the manufacturer's warranty; on used cars the warranty is in addition to the dealer's warranty. Additional warranties usually vary from one to five years and from 12,000 to 50,000 miles, depending on the age of the car and the amount you want to pay for this additional protection.

Some newer used cars are still under the manufacturer's warranty. Be sure to examine the details of the warranty, since some of them are not transferable. Other warranties require a fee for the transfer or limit certain coverage, and some warranties must be validated in a special way in order to be transferred. Read the entire warranty *before* you buy the car, and remember that a warranty is only as good as the dealer who issues it.

2

Financing a Car

Most people who buy new or used cars finance at least part of the cost. Interest charges for financing will vary and depend on several things, such as:

1. Who is lending you the money and for how long
2. The age of the car
3. The type of loan
4. Your credit rating and your present circumstances
5. The legal limits that may be charged

All lending agencies do not charge the same rates. Shop around for financing the same way you shop for the best price when you buy groceries or other commodities; the savings will make it worthwhile. Shop for financing *before* you buy the car.

Here are some sources of financing and their features:

Source	Features
Credit union	One of the lowest rates. Available only to members.
Savings and loan association	Loans available to holders of savings accounts.
Bank	Loans available to holders of savings accounts. Installment loans available to people with good credit ratings.
Car dealer	Convenient, but usually costs more than the other sources, since the dealer often sells your contract to a bank or finance company.

Your life insurance company	Low-cost loan. You may borrow up to the cash value of your policy.
Auto loan companies, such as G.M.A.C. (General Motors Acceptance Corporation), Ford Motor Credit Company, Chrysler Credit Corporation, General Finance Corporation, C.I.T. (Consumer Investment Trust), Financial Service, Inc., Commercial Credit Corporation	Easily obtained, convenient. Competitive with most other finance companies and banks.
Finance and loan companies	Easily obtained, comparatively high interest.

Ask the credit source for the *Annual Percentage Rate* (APR), formerly called the "true annual interest." APR is stated as a percentage, such as 14 percent. Federal law requires that it must be calculated according to a formula set up by the government, which is computed consistently by all lending institutions. APR is calculated on the unpaid balance over the time period of the loan. For example, a $1,000 debt at 11 percent APR costs about $60 in finance charges if paid in a year. A $1,000 debt at 14.5 percent APR costs about $85 in interest charges if paid in a year. Similarly, $3,000 at 11 percent APR costs about $541 if paid in three years; and $3,000 at 14.5 percent APR costs about $721 if paid in three years.

Compare the APR from several credit sources. Not only will it vary from bank to bank, and from credit union to finance company, but the same finance company (for example, G.M.A.C. or C.I.T.) charges often will vary from one automobile dealer to another. Since the dealer usually sells the credit contract to a finance company, he will not deliver the car to you until he is certain the finance company will buy the contract.

State law sets the maximum interest that can be charged on autos, which is determined by the age of the car. The older the car, the higher the finance charges can be, since the older car involves more risk to the lender that he will not recover his money.

Another thing to inquire about is the *total charge*. Besides APR, other charges may be doc (documentary) stamps, office expense, credit investigation, recording fees, title, tag, tax, and similar costs. On the buyer's order form there may be a printed fee listing one or more of the above items.

Some buyers accept the services offered by the "friendly" auto dealer, who will obtain financing and even car insurance. All the buyer has to do is sign on the dotted line and pay so much a month. This is the *easy* way to finance a car, but it is also one of the most expensive.

The federal Truth-in-Lending law, which became effective July 1, 1969, requires that you be told the cost of credit before you sign for the loan. This law also requires that all details be stated clearly and that you receive a copy of the contract when you sign it. All blanks should be filled in or crossed out in the contract.

When you shop for financing, find out how many payments you have to make, of how much, and for how long. Ask what happens to you if the payment is late; will you be charged a late fee or is the car repossessed? When you finance a car requiring monthly payments, you will not be billed each month the way you are billed for electricity, telephone, water, or gas. One young lady who financed a car almost had the car repossessed and her credit rating ruined when she did not make the monthly payments. The reason she had not sent a payment, she said, was that she had not received a bill.

It is usually possible to have credit life insurance included in your credit contract. This type of insurance pays the unpaid balance of the loan if you die before the loan is paid. If your family is not covered by enough insurance, credit life insurance is a good investment.

Be certain that you know the terms of a conditional sales contract or installment loan contract. Read the fine print. You will have possession of the car, but you must comply with all provisions of the contract. Usually you will have to agree to the following:

1. Make monthly payments until the loan is fully paid
2. Carry collision insurance until the loan is paid
3. Not sell the car until it is paid for
4. Be responsible for all damages
5. Keep the lender informed if your address changes

If you do not meet your regular payments or fail to carry out any other part of the contract, one of two things may happen. The entire amount of the loan can become due at once, or the car can be repossessed and sold at auction by the holder of the loan. In some states, if the car does not bring enough money to pay off the loan and the expenses of repossession—such as court costs and lawyers' fees—you will have to pay the balance. You will no doubt be sued if you refuse to pay.

3

Car Insurance

Insurance for your car is no longer a luxury; it is an absolute necessity. The majority of states require owners to carry liability insurance. Whether your state requires car insurance or not, you should have enough liability insurance to protect you from the consequences (law suits, bills to pay, and the like) of any damage, injuries, or destruction that might result from an accident. Other types of coverage are also available; these provisions are usually optional and depend on what you want and the amount you can afford to pay.

Insurance companies write many different kinds of car insurance and costs vary from company to company, so it pays to shop around. Though most states have a regulatory agency that oversees and approves car insurance rates, rates still vary in a given state. Other criteria that enter into the rate structure are the city, county, or area where you live, as well as the age(s) of the driver(s).

If you do not yet own a car but plan to buy one, call an insurance agent to get the rates his company offers. Choose the options and amounts you want and then call several other companies selling car insurance to compare prices. Buying insurance cannot be postponed; you need insurance *immediately* when you sign the papers and drive the car.

If you already own a car and are planning to trade it in, the new car usually will be automatically covered by your insurance policy for several days, to give you plenty of time to notify your insurance agent of the change in vehicles. Call your insurance representative to verify this fact *before* you trade cars.

Many new- and used-car dealers offer a "package" plan of car insurance (as well as car financing) at the time of purchase. All you have to do is make one inclusive payment each month. What a nice dealer he is to arrange car insurance and financing for you, saving you

17

a lot of trouble and bother! Hold it! You may be paying a dear price
for the time and effort saved. In some states it is not legal for an auto
dealer to give you complete coverage, and you will have to buy liability insurance somewhere else. Shop and compare insurance costs;
you will probably find out that an insurance company's rates are
cheaper.

INSURANCE PROVISIONS

Auto insurance has several different provisions or choices. Buy the
policy that gives you the coverage you want.

Liability

Liability coverage is usually written in three numbers: for example
15/30/10. The first number indicates that the company is liable up to
$15,000 per accident for any bodily injury to one person who is not in
your car. The second number states the company liability for bodily
injury to others who are not in your car, which in this case is $30,000
maximum for each accident. The last number indicates the company's
liability for property damage, in this case up to $10,000 per accident.
Some states require a minimum liability coverage of 15/30/10. The
company will pay no more than the liability amount in your policy, and
you will have to pay the additional difference if your car causes personal
injury or property damage and the court awards more than the company is liable for. For this reason, many automobile owners decide to
buy more than the minimum required by law, such as 100/300/50
($100,000/$300,000/$50,000). Increasing your liability insurance to
higher limits is relatively inexpensive, considering the possible consequences. Carry enough liability insurance to safeguard your future
earnings and to protect your accumulation of property and valuables.

PIP

This word stands for "personal injury protection" and refers to medical expenses resulting from bodily injury plus loss of income. The
coverage includes you and any member of your family residing in your
household, whether as a passenger in a car or as a pedestrian.

Uninsured Motorist

Even though your state requires all car owners to carry insurance, you could be hit by an uninsured motorist from your state or another state, or by a hit-and-run driver. You can have a provision in your policy that covers injuries to the driver, any passengers riding in the car, and any household family member, either as a passenger in any car or as a pedestrian. However, the uninsured motorist provision does not cover property damage.

Comprehensive Physical Damage

This part of your policy applies to damage to your car, with certain exclusions. Glass breakage, storm and wind damage, fire, theft, vandalism, flood, riot, and collision with an animal are examples of hazards that are covered; whereas a collision with another car, normal wear and tear, or freezing are not.

Collision

Collision insurance pays for damages to your car caused by a collision with another vehicle or an object. The damages to your car are also covered if your car overturns, for example by skidding, even though it did not collide with an object. Most collision coverage is purchased on a $50-, $100-, or $200-deductible basis, which means you have to pay the first $50, $100, or $200 of the cost of repair. Obviously, $100-deductible collision coverage will cost you less than $50-deductible collision coverage. Most owners do not have full collision coverage because the cost is prohibitive. Collision insurance covers only damage to your car, not injuries or damage to the property of others.

Other Provisions

A variety of other provisions are available, including emergency road service, personal effects coverage (goods stolen from the car), and death indemnity coverage.

NO-FAULT INSURANCE

Approximately one-third of the states have adopted some form of no-fault insurance. Increasing costs of automobile insurance have contributed to the adoption of no-fault insurance in an effort to keep rates down. Because studies show that legal costs in accidents are a major expense to insurance companies, their reduction or elimination saves the companies money, which results in lower costs to the insurance buyer. Basically, no-fault insurance means that when the damage done by the accident does not exceed certain limits set by a state, persons involved in the accident *cannot* use legal means to determine who was at fault. No-fault insurance is constantly being revised and modified from state to state; your insurance agent can explain the current regulations in your state.

BUYING AUTOMOBILE INSURANCE

Remember to shop for insurance the way you shop for a tangible object, such as a house or a car; the effort will save you money. Friends can often tell you their experiences with companies regarding fairness and promptness in settling claims; your chamber of commerce or Better Business Bureau will have a list of reputable companies. If you travel, find out which companies have representatives or a provision for handling claims in the states where you expect to be.

4

Things You Need to Have With You

You cannot anticipate and prepare for every emergency that could arise while you are driving, but for driving around town and on the highway, carrying certain items will not only save you an occasional inconvenience but will help to ensure your safety. In an emergency some of them will be extremely valuable.

Let us begin with the things you normally will have:

1. Keep the _Owner's Manual_ in the glove compartment where you can get it easily for reference.

2. Be sure you have a _spare tire_ that is inflated. Check the spare tire when you check the air pressure of the other tires (see Chapter 12, Four Regular Checks). Then when you need the spare it will be ready for use.

3. It goes without saying that you should have your _operator's license_ and _insurance policy information_ in your wallet or purse. Most states require the _auto registration_ to be with you or in the car.

I recommend you have these additional things:

4. Keep a _pocket tire gauge_ in the glove compartment where it is dry and safe from damage.

5. Buy _jumper cables,_ and be sure to get the large, heavy-duty cables made of copper wire (see Chapter 6, Electricity and Your Car).

6. You should have a _flashlight._ Keep the flashlight in a handy place where it is easy to find, such as the glove compartment. Flashlight batteries deteriorate whether used or not, so check your flashlight every month or so and replace the batteries when they get weak.

7. A large (about 22 inches) _X wrench_ is useful for changing a tire, particularly if you have very little strength (see Chapter 17, Tips on Easy Tasks).

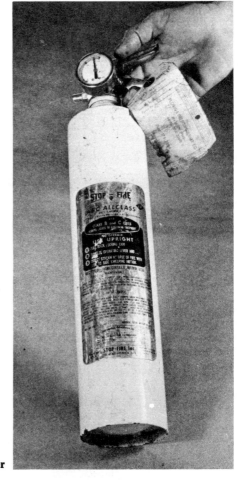

Fire extinguisher

8. Every car should carry a *fire extinguisher*. The cost is small compared to the savings if a fire should start. Be sure to get the proper kind when you buy an extinguisher. The so-called "salt-shaker" type, which you shake to put chemicals on the fire, is not good; you can-

not get close enough to the fire for the extinguisher to be effective. You need an extinguisher that has the UL (Underwriters Laboratories, Inc.) approval. Buy a portable extinguisher with gauge—about a two-and-one-half-pound, pressurized, dry-chemical, all-purpose extinguisher for class A, B, and C fires. This means it will be effective on fabric fires, such as the upholstery (class A), oil or gasoline fires (class B), and electrical fires (class C). If you cannot locate such an extinguisher, another excellent one is similar but is approved only for class B and C fires. The extinguisher can be recharged at low cost (about $5 to $6) at a company selling fire extinguisher equipment. A pressurized dry-chemical extinguisher only needs recharging after use or when the pressure gauge is down.

9. Keep a *first-aid kit* under the front seat or in the trunk. An approved first-aid kit from your drugstore or safety organization will do. Johnson & Johnson is one of the reputable pharmaceutical companies producing an excellent first-aid emergency kit for autos.

Check your first-aid kit and add any of these things that are not in it: first-aid booklet, sterile gauze pads, roll of bandage cloth, small pair of scissors, burn ointment, merthiolate, sterile cotton, cotton-tipped swabs, adhesive bandages, adhesive tape, ammonia inhalants, package of needles (useful for removing splinters), a snake-bite kit, and syrup of ipecac (one ounce, to induce vomiting in certain kinds of poisoning, available from your druggist without a prescription). The commercial first-aid emergency kit I bought for my car contained many useful items but did not have several things I wanted. I removed several duplicate bandages and compresses to make room for the additional things I needed.

There is no need to dwell on the value of a first-aid kit in your car. Families who drive to the beach or to the woods for camping, picnicking, hunting, fishing, and hiking will have occasion to use the first-aid kit. Accidents occur every day on the road; and practically every driver will either be involved in an accident, or be on the scene of an accident at some time.

10. In addition to a flashlight, it is useful to have a *heavy-duty spotlight* with a red flasher attached. The spotlight is much brighter than a flashlight and has many uses on the road. If you have a flat tire or other emergency, put the spotlight on the road by your car and use the red flasher to warn other drivers. Flares are also useful for shunting oncoming traffic away from a stopped car.

11. It is useful to have *two wheel blocks* when changing a wheel with a flat tire to chock up the opposing tires, though you can always

use two rocks. Blocks 4 × 4 × 8 inches are adequate, and you can either buy or make them.

12. A *pressurized can* to inflate a flat tire is handy. Sometimes a tire with a slow leak will go down overnight. This can will give the tire enough pressure so you can drive to a service station to get the trouble repaired. Thus the pressurized can saves you from having to call a service truck or put on the spare yourself. Cans are available at auto parts stores.

13. You should always have an extra *quart of oil* of the brand and grade you normally use.

14. Carry a plastic *gallon container of coolant*. A plastic milk container is satisfactory to carry the liquid, which can prevent your being stranded if the car's engine overheats because of too little coolant.

15. Keep *spare fuses* of each size in your car.

16. A *spare fan belt* is good insurance, especially if you are starting on a long trip, and particularly if you own a foreign car. Take with you the *tools* needed to install the new fan belt. I recommend replacing all belts every two years or 25,000 miles. Keep unbroken old belts in the trunk to use as spares.

17. It is important to have a *spare car door key* in your wallet or purse. Some drivers tie the spare key under the car or use a commercial magnetic box to hide the key underneath the car; I do not recommend the magnetic boxes, as they are easily dislodged. If you have ever locked your keys inside the car, you know the feeling; one such incident will convince a driver to keep a spare key.

18. Carry with you *road maps* of your home state and other areas where you are likely to travel.

19. See Chapter 19, Hints for Cold Climates, for several additional *cold-weather items* you need if you drive in a northern state in the winter.

20. Keep *this book* in your glove compartment for easy reference.

5

Let's Look Under the Hood

Obviously, to look under the engine hood you first have to raise it, which is sometimes not so simple a task as it sounds. The engine is in the front on most American and foreign cars. First look under the dashboard to the left of the steering column for a hood release device; that is where they are positioned on most cars, but they come in a variety of shapes and are sometimes located at the front of the hood. The next place to try is at the front of the car; reach your fingers through an opening in the grill and feel around for a release lever. The Owner's Manual contains both the location and instructions (it may be indexed as "bonnet" in foreign car manuals), but if you have a problem with it, stop at a service station or ask the dealer where you purchased the car for help. Once you have located the release and raised the hood, do it several times until you memorize how it is done.

Interior hood release

There are three kinds of hoods, varying in their location and the way they open. The most common hood is located at the front end of the car, is hinged near the windshield, opens at the front, and has two catches. After the first catch is released, the hood raises perhaps an inch, and the second catch must be activated to raise the hood completely. (That second catch is there as a safety measure to prevent a hood from being accidentally released and blown back while the car is in motion.) Another kind of hood located at the front end of the car has the hinges at the front with the opening near the windshield. This type of hood has only one release. The third kind of hood is located at the rear of the car and is called a "motor lid" on a VW Beetle or bus, some Fiats, some Renaults, Corvairs, and some other cars. With some foreign cars that have rear engines, for instance the VW Beetle, the trunk (or "boot") is in the front of the car and the catch release is in the glove compartment.

A raised hood, incidentally, is the universal distress signal, so if you break down on the road raise the hood and tie a handkerchief to the radio antenna. While you are trying to figure out the trouble, perhaps some kind soul will stop or will send help.

When you first look under the hood the vast array of wires, hoses, and unfamiliar items will almost overwhelm you. Take heart, you are not supposed to know what each and every part is and how it performs or how to fix it. You are going to learn simple repair, proper care, and preventive maintenance; as you learn the function of a few parts and how to care for them, the engine will not look mystifying any more. The more you learn about the engine the more you will appreciate the marvelous arrangement of coordinated devices that perform at your command and operate precisely with all parts synchronized to do the best job.

Under the hood, Volkswagen

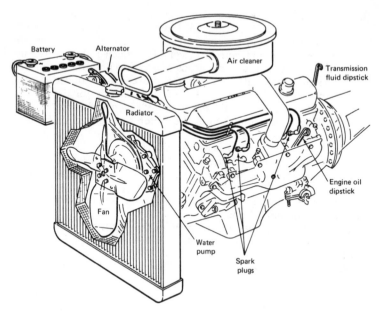

Under the hood, schematic of American car

Under the hood, typical American car

Here is a simple explanation of how a four-cycle gasoline engine—the kind found in most American and foreign cars—works. The source of the horsepower in a car is a series of four to eight pistons, which are located in the engine and housed in cylinders. Each piston moves up and down in its cylinder, and by means of a connecting rod this movement causes the crankshaft to rotate; this movement, in turn, is transferred to the wheels themselves. The source of energy for the pistons is a combustible mixture of air and gasoline which is fed by the carburetor to the cylinder that houses the piston and ignited there by a spark from the spark plug. The carburetor mixes air and gas in correct proportions to form a vapor that will burn rapidly.

In a four-cycle engine, it takes four strokes of a piston, two up and two down, to complete a full series. Then the procedure starts all over again.

Stroke 1. The piston moves *down,* drawing the fuel-air mixture into the cylinder from the carburetor.

Stroke 2. The piston goes *up,* compressing the mixture.

Stroke 3. A spark ignites the mixture, which burns rapidly, forcing the piston *down.*

Stroke 4. The piston moves *up,* expelling the burned gases.

Four-cycle gasoline engine

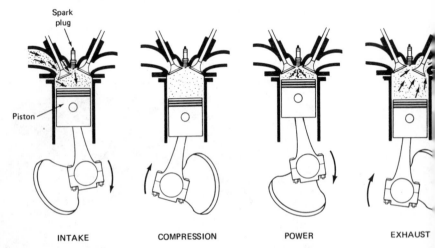

INTAKE   COMPRESSION   POWER   EXHAUST

In addition to compression, three vital elements are necessary to make the engine run: fuel, air, and electricity. If the engine turns over but will not start, or coughs to a stop while you are driving, the most likely problem is that you are out of gasoline. Even if you filled the tank yesterday, that does not always mean you have plenty today; maybe a thief stole your gas during the night.

The second item—air—is always present, and you will never have to worry about running out of it. A properly balanced mixture of air and gas is fed by the carburetor to the engine. Though an incorrect mixture will increase fuel consumption, it probably will not prevent the car from starting.

That leaves electricity, and now we have to do a little trouble-shooting. When the starter will not turn the engine over, the lights will not burn, and the horn will not blow, then there is no electricity flowing from the battery to the starter. Either the battery is dead (out of juice) or the terminals are corroded. If there is some white or gray-ish mush on the terminals, loosen the cables with a wrench or pliers, remove them, and clean off the terminals. Then replace and tighten the cables; that may correct the problem. If not, you will probably need jumper cables and a helper battery to get going (see Chapter 17, Tips on Easy Tasks). If your battery has life and spins the engine but it does not start it running, then you have more serious problems in the electrical system, such as points, condenser, plugs, plug wires, or distributor—trouble that may be beyond your ability to correct.

UNDER THE HOOD

As you look under the hood, you can identify the *belts* on the pulleys. These drive the fan and alternator (generator on some foreign cars). Belts also drive some of the optional equipment, such as an air conditioner compressor and power steering pump.

You will also see an array of insulated wires coming from a round device called the *distributor*. The distributor sends electricity over the various wires to the *spark plugs* in the proper sequence. The wires spread from the distributor to each of the spark plugs in octopus fashion. Each cylinder has one spark plug; if you drive a four-cylinder car, then you have four spark plugs. A V-8 of any make has eight spark plugs, four on each side of the engine. An electric spark jumps across the electrodes of the spark plug and ignites the fuel-air mixture.

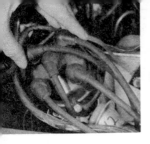

Distributor

Air cleaner filter

The *air cleaner* is usually a large, round, canlike item, most often located above the *carburetor* right over the engine. Inside the air cleaner is a paper filter that removes dust, dirt, and other objectionable particles from the air entering the carburetor. This paper filter must be replaced when it gets dirty; refer to your Owner's Manual for suggestions on how often to check or replace the air filter. The carburetor mixes the gas and air in the proper proportions to form a vapor that will burn in the engine.

A *plastic container* holds water or water and chemicals to clean the windshield. Detergent or a special cleaning solution can be added to the water to do a better cleaning job. In winter, use a special solution containing antifreeze, or add a deicer to the water in the container to prevent freezing.

The *alternator* is a round device approximately 6 inches in diameter and 6 inches thick. It has a pulley that is belt-driven and it produces electricity to keep the battery charged. About fifteen years ago some American car manufacturers started using alternators instead of generators. Older VW's have a generator, but recently foreign car manufacturers switched to alternators and now practically all American and foreign cars have alternators. The alternator is more efficient than the generator and has a higher capacity than a generator of equal size. When the dashboard alternator warning light (GEN) comes on, the most likely problem is that the drive belt has broken. Pull over to the side of the road and let the engine idle while you open the hood. If the drive belt is broken and *the fan is turning,* close the hood and drive to the nearest service station or garage for repairs. Do not turn the engine off! Your battery may be run down and may not start the car again. While driving for help, turn off the radio, air conditioner, heater, and other electrical equipment to conserve electricity, because the alternator is not replacing the electricity used. If the drive belt is broken and *the fan is not turning,* turn the engine off at once! (On some cars the fan is driven by the same belt that drives the alternator.) You will have to obtain help. With the fan stopped an engine will soon overheat, and expensive damage to the engine may result.

Next find the *radiator,* the large metal container located between the engine and the grill which contains the antifreeze or mixture of antifreeze and water that is used in the cooling process. You will see two rubber *hoses* attached to the radiator, one at the top and one at the bottom. When these hoses get soft or easy to squeeze, they should be replaced, normally about every two years (see Chapter 18, Tips on Medium Tasks). Cars with air-cooled engines do not have radiators; an example is a VW with the engine in the rear.

The proper liquid level in the radiator is extremely important. Your car has either a sealed cooling system or a conventional pressure cooling system (see Chapter 7, The Cooling System). A sealed cooling system has a translucent *plastic container,* which holds the overflow coolant; this is located near the radiator and is connected to it by a hose entering the radiator near the cap.

The *battery* is easy to identify; it resembles a cube in shape, being about 10 inches long, 7 inches wide, and 8 inches deep. The battery is called a storage battery because it provides electricity to start the engine and then is recharged when the engine is running. Two heavy insulated electrical *cables* attach to terminals on the top or on the side of the battery. On the top are six vent caps or lids (except in some new batteries, which never need to have water added). Each vent cap must be removed to check the liquid level in the battery (see Chapter 12, Four Regular Checks).

Radiator

Alternator

Battery

Oil dipstick

Transmission fluid dipstick

Ask the seller to show you where the battery is located if you buy a foreign car, or you may have to hunt for it. For example, some Fiats with rear engines may have the battery under the floor mat of the front trunk. A VW Beetle has the battery under the rear seat; lift up the lower part of the rear seat and you will locate the battery on the passenger side. Most foreign cars have the battery located under the front hood, just as in most American cars.

The *oil dipstick* is used to check the engine oil level and is located on the side of the engine. You can identify it by the loop at the protruding end of the stick, which allows it to be pulled out easily for checking. (To check the level of oil, see Chapter 12, Four Regular Checks.)

If your car has a manual shift, there is only one dipstick under the hood. If you have automatic transmission, there is a *transmission fluid dipstick* to measure the level of the transmission fluid. This dipstick is located at the rear of the engine near the fire wall, the partition that separates the engine compartment from the passenger compartment. This partition is fire-resistant to lessen the danger of fire getting into the passenger compartment from the engine.

You do not normally have to worry about checking the transmission fluid, which is checked when the car is serviced at regular intervals. If for some reason the transmission fluid becomes low, the automatic transmission will be sluggish in shifting. You can have the transmission fluid checked at the nearest garage or service station, or check it yourself (see Chapter 17, Tips on Easy Tasks) and add some fluid if needed.

The items I have named are certainly not all the things found under the hood. But they are the components that are easily seen or located, and the ones you will be concerned with in performing basic auto care. After you can identify these parts, you should check the hood as often as necessary to protect the engine and give you peace of mind, perhaps every two weeks or every 500 miles. This check should include the liquid level in the radiator, the liquid level of the battery, and the level of oil in the engine. In addition, the tire pressure should be checked (see Chapter 12, Four Regular Checks).

6

Electricity and Your Car

Electricity is one of the three things necessary to make the car run.
Electric energy from the storage battery turns an electric motor called
a starter, which starts the engine running by turning it through the
four cycles of a gasoline engine. The battery also provides the electric
spark necessary to ignite the gas-air mixture in the cylinder. Points,
condenser, rotor, coil, ignition wires, alternator, and spark plugs are
other components of the electrical system besides the battery. Some
new cars have an electronic ignition system that does not have any
points to wear out.

BATTERY

The electrical system gets power from the battery, which is recharged by the alternator (generator) while the engine is running. If
the starter sounds sluggish, if the headlights brighten perceptibly when
the engine is raced, or if the engine will not turn over at all, your
battery may need recharging or replacing. Service stations can test
the battery in a short time. It must be replaced if one cell is shorted or
dead. If the battery is still under warranty, see a dealer selling that
brand for an adjustment. You will be charged a pro-rata share of the
cost of a new battery, depending on how many months you used the
battery. The longer the warranty, the less the cost per month of owning
the battery. For instance, a forty-eight-month battery is cheaper to
own per month than a twelve-month battery.

Sometimes lights or other electrical equipment are left on, causing
the battery to become run-down so that it cannot start the car. Normally
this only requires charging the battery at a service station.

An automotive storage battery is made of cells containing positively and negatively charged lead plates covered with a solution of acid and water. This is known as a lead-acid battery. Each cell produces about two volts of electricity. The cells are connected in series, which means the voltage of the individual cells is added to give the total voltage of the battery. A battery with six cells delivers six times two volts or twelve volts of electricity. Each cell is insulated from all the others. To learn how to check the battery, see Chapter 12, Four Regular Checks.

Every car battery should be secured firmly by clamps or brackets. Sometimes corrosion or breakage causes these fasteners to become loose and the battery slides around when the car is moving. Cables can pull loose, acid can spill, and vibration and bouncing can loosen materials that pile up in the bottom of the battery, shorting it and drastically reducing its life. Take the car to a garage or service station immediately and have the battery anchored securely.

A new type of battery appeared on the market in 1975 that has no caps and never needs to have water added. It produces less corrosion than the conventional battery. Delco is one company that makes this battery; some new cars come equipped with it.

CORROSION

It is normal for a white powdery substance to collect on the battery terminals and the metal clamps that hold the battery secure. This is corrosion. Corrosion on battery terminals may act in a mysterious way. Let's say you have driven to the post office and are inside for five minutes. When you return to the car everything is dead—the starter will not turn the engine over, the lights will not burn, and the horn will not blow. What has happened? Corrosion has struck again!

Corrosion behaves as an insulator, and when it gets between the battery terminal and the cable clamp it can stop the flow of electricity. And all this can happen in just five minutes! Sounds unbelievable, but it is true. You can prevent corrosion from giving you problems. See Chapter 17, Tips on Easy Tasks, to find out how.

JUMPER CABLES

I recommend that every driver keep a set of jumper cables in the trunk of the car at all times. It's good insurance. I hope you will never need jumper cables; but if an emergency arises and you use them to help yourself or someone else you will be glad you had them.

First let me tell you what kind of jumper cables to buy. Get the heavy-duty type made of thick, insulated copper wire. The copper wire is easily identified by the copper color. You can expect to pay about $10 to $15 at an auto discount store for a good set of jumper cables. Beware the sale fliers that some stores distribute advertising a special low price of $2.98 for jumper cables. These cheap cables have aluminum (white) wire, which is not as good a conductor as copper. The cables are small, sometimes no larger in diameter than an ordinary pencil. The modern automobile engine needs considerable electric energy to rotate it and provide the spark for ignition at the same time. The purchasers of inferior jumper cables often have been disappointed because the cables did not carry enough electricity to start a car. So remember this word of advice, and if you buy cables get a set that will do the job in time of need.

For information on using jumper cables to jump-start your car, see Chapter 17, Tips on Easy Tasks.

SPARK PLUGS

Spark plugs are an important part of the electrical system, and they do wear out. They become pitted, corroded, and inefficient, and usually are changed when the engine is tuned about every 10,000 miles. A person who wants to change his own plugs can get a service manual from his car dealer to help him.

Spark plug

Insulated
electrode

Gap

Grounded
electrode

SPARK PLUG

A spark plug has an insulated electrode in the center and a grounded electrode attached to the side. The high voltage from the distributor jumps the gap between the two spark plug electrodes, producing a spark inside the combustion chamber of the engine. This spark ignites the fuel-air mixture at the proper time and the engine runs.

FUSES

Fuses protect electric motors and wiring from overheating. Your Owner's Manual will tell you where fuses are located in your car. For information on changing fuses, see Chapter 17, Tips on Easy Tasks.

OTHER PARTS OF THE ELECTRICAL SYSTEM

You can do other things to maintain your electrical system; for instance, you can replace burned-out light bulbs. To learn how, see Chapter 17, Tips on Easy Tasks.

7

The Cooling System

Every car has a cooling system. Some foreign cars, such as rear-engine VW's, have an air-cooled system that is relatively trouble-free, but most American-made cars and many foreign cars have a combination liquid and air cooling system. Unfortunately, all the heat produced by an internal-combustion engine cannot be utilized as energy, and the excess heat above the normal operating temperature must be removed or else it will damage and even destroy the engine.

Overheating of the engine is a problem in all areas of the country, but especially in those sections where summer temperatures are high. Simple care and maintenance of your cooling system will help you avoid overheating problems.

The cooling system is basically simple. A conventional system consists of a radiator with cores through which water circulates to allow maximum air contact and heat removal; other components are a fan, a water pump that is belt-driven on the same shaft as the fan, a thermostat, hoses, coolant, and a pressure radiator cap. Most cars manufactured before 1972 have a conventional cooling system.

Some newer cars have a closed cooling system. In addition to the parts that comprise the conventional system, the closed system has a plastic see-through container and a hose that leads from the container to the top of the radiator near the cap. As the liquid in the radiator becomes hot and expands, it overflows from the radiator into the reserve container. Conversely, as the radiator cools, the liquid is drawn back into it. A closed cooling system has a sign on the radiator cap that says "Do Not Open." Follow these instructions; you should not open the radiator cap.

Keep the outside of the radiator clean. Remove bugs, leaves, and trash from the front of the radiator. Check the fan belts. If they are obviously quite worn or frazzled, go ahead and replace them (see Chapter 18, Tips on Medium Tasks). Do not wait until they break or you may be severely inconvenienced. When preparing for a long trip, take spare belts with you and tools for replacing any broken belts.

THE COOLANT

The coolant is an important part of the cooling system. Refer to your Owner's Manual to find out what coolant is recommended for your car. The antifreeze-and-water mixture freezes at a lower temperature and boils at a higher temperature than water. Always use permanent type (ethylene glycol base) antifreeze. The colder the temperature the more antifreeze you will need (see Chapter 19, Hints for Cold Climates). Even in mild climates, some of the newer cars require a fifty-fifty mixture of antifreeze and water all the time.

The coolant level in your cooling system should be checked every two weeks or every 500 miles or before a long trip (see Chapter 12, Four Regular Checks).

ADDING WATER

The water you put in your radiator ideally should be free of alkali or other minerals. Since most service stations use tap water, you may want to be on the safe side and use rainwater or distilled water in the radiator. (Rainwater does not contain minerals, because it has not passed through channels in the earth picking up these materials.)

FLUSHING THE COOLING SYSTEM

Every two years your car's cooling system should be drained, flushed out with clean water, and filled with new antifreeze. You can have this done at a service station or do it yourself (see Chapter 18, Tips on Medium Tasks).

THE HOSES

The two primary hoses for your cooling system are extremely important. One hose leads from the engine to the top of the radiator and the other leads from the engine to the bottom of the radiator. These hoses will rot with ordinary use. When they become soft and flabby (usually after about two years), it is time they were changed. Changing the hoses should coincide with flushing out the cooling system. If you want to change the hoses yourself, see Chapter 18, Tips on Medium Tasks.

OVERHEATING

When an engine overheats, the temperature indicator or idiot light on the dashboard lights up. Stop immediately! With luck, the engine has not yet been damaged but continued driving surely will damage it. Open the hood and look for a broken fan belt. If the fan belt and fan are in good condition, the coolant may be low. Do not open the radiator cap of a hot engine. Use a hose to spray water on the radiator to cool it before opening the radiator cap. If the coolant is low, crank the engine and let it idle while adding coolant. Never add cold liquid to the radiator of a hot engine that is not running. Doing this may damage the engine.

If the fan belt is neither loose nor broken, and the liquid coolant level is correct, then the next most likely problem is the thermostat.

A thermostat is a small round device, about two inches in diameter—or slightly larger than a silver dollar—which is mounted under a metal

Thermostat

bracket where the top radiator hose attaches to the engine. See Chapter 18, Tips on Medium Tasks, if you want to replace the thermostat yourself; otherwise have it replaced with a new one of the proper size (see Chapter 16, Ripoffs). When the engine is started cold the thermostat is closed; the water pump sends coolant to the engine block to be heated, and as the engine comes rapidly up to proper operating temperature (about 190° F.), the thermostat opens. This allows the heated liquid from the engine to circulate through the radiator, where it is cooled. The movement of the car and the rotating fan cause cool air to pass through openings in the radiator, cooling the liquid, which then flows around the engine block and other engine parts picking up heat again. In this circulating process the thermostat helps to maintain the proper engine temperature by opening and closing. Proper engine temperature results in better gas mileage, better acceleration, and less engine wear.

If the engine still overheats, the trouble may be that the radiator core is full of rust and corrosion and must be boiled in a cleaning solution or rodded out. This is a job for the professional radiator shop. Another possible, though remote, problem is a defective fan clutch, in which case the pulley turns but the fan does not.

QUESTION: Is the cooling system designed to keep the engine as cool as possible? No, it keeps the engine at the *proper* operating temperature. Always remember that overheating of the engine leads to untold troubles, all of which can result in expensive repair bills. Obviously, you should make every effort to see that your engine does not overheat.

PRESSURE RADIATOR CAPS

Modern cooling systems are under pressure and use pressure type radiator caps. Your coolant will be lost if the cap leaks. The radiator cap is designed so that it has a pressure-relief valve. After the pressure in the radiator reaches a certain point, the pressure-relief valve is actuated, and some of the pressure is released. When you check the coolant level in a conventional system, make sure you replace the cap tightly.

WATER PUMP AND FAN

The water pump should last a long time, but eventually it will wear out and need replacement. Leaks and/or squeaky noises are symptoms that the water pump is approaching the time of trouble. The only thing you can do to prolong the life of your water pump is to keep anti-freeze or a rust preventive solution in the cooling system at all times. If you have an older car that does not require year-round antifreeze, you may decide to flush the cooling system in the spring and put water alone in the radiator. In this case be certain to add a can of rust preventative, which will lubricate the water pump as well as help prevent rust. Antifreeze also helps prevent rust and lubricates the water pump, so if you leave antifreeze in your cooling system year round, you do not have to add rust preventative.

The engines of some modern cars, such as the Chevrolet Vega and Ford Courier, have aluminum blocks. The proper concentration of the antifreeze recommended by the manufacturer is especially important in aluminum-block engines to prevent corrosion.

The fan normally lasts a long time and seldom gives trouble. The fan belt may break, but you can have a mechanic replace the belt or you can do it yourself (see Chapter 18, Tips on Medium Tasks).

8

Brakes, Steering, and Shocks

BRAKES

From the standpoint of safety, the brakes are the most important feature of your car. Properly functioning brakes—along with tires, steering, and lighting—help ensure your safety. If I were helping anyone select a used car, I would emphasize the items pertaining to safety in preference to anything else.

Be conscious of your car's brake action and notice any perceptible changes, such as the pedal depressing farther than usual, squeaky noises, or the wheels pulling to one side when you apply the brakes. Correct any trouble at once. Do not delay! Driving with questionable brakes that might fail in an emergency is not worth the risk.

The two kinds of brakes found on cars are drum brakes and disc brakes; either kind may be power assisted. Drum brakes have been used for many years. Such a brake consists of a round drum mounted parallel to the wheel, turning as the wheel turns. Inside the drum are two "shoes," each lined with asbestos on the side facing the drum. When the brakes are applied these shoes press against the inside of the drum, which causes the wheel to slow or stop turning. The asbestos linings eventually wear thin and must be replaced. Brakes should be relined when the lining gets thin and before the rivets are exposed, otherwise grooves will be worn in the smooth surface of the drum. If this happens, it is necessary to have the drum turned on a lathe, necessitating additional expense.

Disc brakes are a newer development. Higher priced cars often come equipped with disc brakes on all four wheels; some less expensive cars have disc brakes on the front wheels and drum brakes on the rear

Drum brake

Disc brake

wheels. Disc brakes are definitely superior to drum brakes; in actual use the discs dissipate heat much more rapidly. Heat is the enemy of brakes, causing wear to brake linings and pads.

A disc brake is basically a round disc, similar to a phonograph record, mounted parallel to the wheel. Pads on both sides press against the disc when the brakes are applied. This type of brake is much more dependable and has less danger of fading or giving way. Safety authorities estimate that 60 percent of stopping is accomplished by the front wheels, which is why models equipped with only two disc brakes carry them on the front wheels.

Here is a simplified description of brakes and how they work. When you push the foot pedal, pressure is applied to the brakes on all four wheels through hollow lines containing brake fluid. One line leads to the two front-wheel brakes and the other to the two rear-wheel brakes. If one line fails the other will work, so you will have brakes on two wheels at least. The braking system was designed this way as a safety feature.

Get a competent mechanic to inspect your brakes periodically for wear. The frequency of this inspection depends on terrain, traffic conditions, and your driving habits. See your Owner's Manual for suggestions on when to have the brakes inspected. An average driver with good driving habits on terrain that is fairly level should be able to go 10,000 miles before having brakes inspected. The results of the inspection will help you decide when to have the brakes relined or how soon they should be inspected again. The mechanic should not charge to make this inspection for you, especially if he knows he will get the job if any work is needed on the brakes. The front-wheel brakes get the most wear and will need relining sooner than the rear-wheel brakes. If you are told that the brakes need relining, find out if the mechanic means all the brakes or those on the front wheels only.

A reservoir mounted under the hood on the fire wall holds a supply of brake fluid. The level of brake fluid in this reservoir should be checked every time the car is serviced (to do it yourself, see Chapter 17, Tips on Easy Tasks).

On many cars manufactured since about 1970, the brakes are self-adjusting, designed to eliminate periodic brake adjustments. Cars with drum brakes adjust themselves if you apply the brakes while the car is moving backward; disc brake adjustment is made automatically with each brake application. Refer to your Owner's Manual to learn how your brakes are adjusted.

Some drivers carelessly drive along with one foot resting lightly on the brake pedal, or they brake with their left foot (particularly on cars that have automatic transmission). Both practices are dangerous and cause unnecessary wear. Do not fall into these habits.

The emergency brake is a hand-actuated lever or a foot pedal usually located to the left in the driving compartment, though sometimes it is to the right of the driver's seat. Your emergency brake is just that —it is for emergencies and should stop the car. It should also be used to hold the car when you park on an incline. Emergency brakes stop only the rear wheels. Have your emergency brake adjusted immediately if it is not operating properly.

Power brakes have a vacuum booster that aids the braking system, enabling you to stop with much less foot pressure than you would have to use without this feature. When you push the foot pedal, you should have full braking power when the pedal is about 1½ to 2 inches from the floorboard. Have your brakes checked and adjusted at once if the pedal goes down farther than that.

STEERING

The steering system is very important for your safety. Normal greasing of the car at regular intervals will help prevent trouble in the steering system. Most of the grease fittings used in a grease (lube) job are located near the front wheels and steering components. See a competent mechanic at once if steering becomes difficult or unusual.

Power steering makes for effortless steering. A belt drives the power steering pump, and it will wear out eventually. You can replace belts yourself (see Chapter 18, Tips on Medium Tasks). When the car is serviced, the lubricant level in the power steering pump will be checked. See Chapter 17, Tips on Easy Tasks, if you want to check the lubricant level yourself.

SHOCK ABSORBERS

A shock absorber is located near each wheel, thus every car has four shocks. Sometimes the shocks are mounted within large springs. When the wheel strikes an object, such as a railroad track, a brick, or a pothole, the springs help absorb some of the bounce and keep the car from jolting the passengers. The shocks are stabilizers that prevent excessive bouncing and keep the car from swaying too much when it goes around a curve. Shocks also help support any weight placed on a car.

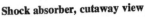

Shock absorber, cutaway view

A shock absorber is not complicated. A piston inside a cylinder compresses air as the piston moves up and does the same thing as it moves down. The resistance of the air being compressed causes the piston to move only when considerable force is applied.

Contrary to what some people believe, a shock absorber is not full of oil. It contains only a small amount of oil to form an airtight seal between the piston and the cylinder.

Shocks generally do not wear out all at once. They gradually get weaker and weaker until it is necessary to replace them. Symptoms of worn shocks that need replacing are:

1. Excessive bouncing when your car crosses over railroad tracks or bumps, and delay in returning to a stable condition.
2. Extreme leaning on curves.
3. The wheel barely clears the ground when the bumper jack is raised all the way. (If the wheel will not clear the ground, you can solve this problem temporarily by placing the bumper jack on a block of wood, but do not delay in getting the shocks replaced.)
4. The front fender sinks low when an average person (about 150 pounds) sits on it.
5. The front tires show wear in the form of pits spaced at intervals on the tire tread.

When you know that one or more shock absorbers (often those on the front) are weak and need replacing, have all four replaced. They have all seen the same number of miles and about the same number of bumps.

9

Filters, Fuels, and Lubricants

FILTERS

A car has several filters that are important to the life of the car. Neglect to replace these filters when they need changing, and you will pay for your negligence in higher operating costs and higher repair bills. Among the filters are the oil filter, the air cleaner, the automatic transmission filter or screen, and the gasoline filter.

OIL FILTER

I suggest you change the oil filter every time the oil is changed. Some Owner's Manuals recommend changing the oil filter every other oil change, but I do not agree. Suppose your engine requires six quarts of oil; if you do not change the filter, it will only take five quarts, since one remains in the filter. When you drain the dirty oil from the engine and put in five quarts of clean oil, the one quart of dirty oil in the filter will mix with the clean oil, giving you six quarts of dirty oil and a dirty filter. This is poor economy. You should change the oil filter each time the oil is changed. You can save money by buying oil filters and oil from a discount house. See Chapter 18, Tips on Medium Tasks, if you want to change your own oil and oil filter, thereby saving even more money.

You can usually get oil filters for foreign cars from a regular auto parts dealer, but if the filters are not available see the foreign car dealer. An air-cooled VW has an oil strainer in place of an oil filter, which may be washed in gasoline or kerosene; the gaskets then have to be replaced.

Oil filter

Oil filter wrench

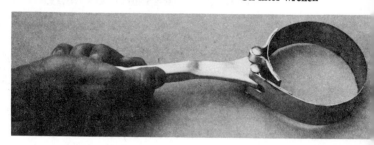

AIR CLEANER FILTER

The air cleaner filter element is made of paper and cannot be cleaned; a dirty element must be replaced. When new, the filter element is perfectly white inside and out. The appearance gets darker as the filter gets clogged with dust, sand, and other foreign matter. Hold the element in front of a bright light to see its condition.

An engine draws air through the air cleaner and gas from the fuel line, and the two are mixed in the carburetor. If the flow of either one is impeded, the engine will draw more of the other, which explains why a dirty air cleaner causes the engine to burn more gas. Changing a dirty air cleaner saves gas and that saves money. You can also save money by buying a replacement air cleaner element and installing it yourself (see Chapter 17, Tips on Easy Tasks).

Comparison of clean and dirty air cleaner filter elements

Some foreign cars, such as the VW Beetle and bus prior to 1975, have oil-bath air filters. Refer to your Owner's Manual for the recommended frequency of checking the oil level and servicing the filter.

AUTOMATIC TRANSMISSION FILTER

One filter that many car owners never see is the automatic transmission filter (sometimes called a screen). Many car owners neglect to have the automatic transmission serviced, and the resulting transmission trouble usually means expensive repair bills. The two most common causes of transmission repairs result from driving the car with insufficient fluid at high speeds or for long distances, and failing to have the transmission serviced at regular intervals. The Owner's Manual of my car, for instance, states that under normal driving conditions the transmission should be serviced every 24,000 miles.

Servicing the transmission involves making adjustments and checking various components, besides changing the fluid and changing or cleaning the filter. Paper filters must be changed, while metal filters need cleaning or changing. Take your car to a transmission repair shop for transmission service and for any repairs that are needed; these are not jobs for the do-it-yourselfer or the average service station.

If your automatic transmission is sluggish in shifting, or will not shift from low gear to a higher gear, the problem may be that the transmission fluid is low. Another symptom is if the engine races during the shifting operation. Have the fluid level checked at once, because continued driving may damage the transmission. Watch for oil spots where you have been parking your car; this kind of leak may indicate trouble with your automatic transmission.

Filter for automatic transmission

GASOLINE FILTER

The gasoline filter is standard equipment on most cars manufactured since about 1970. Located either in the carburetor, on the fuel pump, or somewhere along the gas line to the carburetor, its purpose is to remove or trap water, trash, and sediments that may be in the gasoline. Water can come from condensation in the gas tank or from the service station pump.

There is nothing that you should do about the gasoline filter. If the filter needs cleaning or replacing, a good mechanic will do that when the car is tuned; if he finds foreign matter in the carburetor, he may suggest that you need a supplemental gas filter. Usually this is installed in the line to the carburetor. A warning sign that the gas filter needs replacing is when the engine performs erratically, lunging forward and then holding back.

FUELS

Many American cars made since 1975 require or perform best with unleaded fuel, as do some of the late-model foreign cars. On such cars the opening to the gas tank is smaller than on earlier cars, and the hose nozzle on the unleaded pump at the service station is smaller than the nozzle on the pump with leaded fuel. It is difficult to put leaded gas in a car that requires unleaded gas, and you should not do it. One reason for the unleaded gas requirement is the use of a catalytic converter on the engine, the purpose of which is to decrease the amount of pollutants put into the air by the burning of the fuel in the engine. Using leaded gasoline would soon ruin this catalytic converter, and a replacement would be expensive. Some states with high air pollution levels have special requirements.

Supplemental gas filter

If your American car is a 1974 model or older, it probably uses regular leaded gas, as do most foreign cars. Some large American and foreign cars are designed to use only premium gas. You should use the fuel recommended by your Owner's Manual. An engine that burns regular gas constantly, especially with stop-and-go driving, will accumulate carbon. Fill the tank once with premium gas after four or five tanks of regular gas; then take your car on the highway and drive it at the legal limit for ten miles or so. Many knowledgeable mechanics believe—and there is evidence to support this—that an occasional tank of premium gas will help to clean the engine of excess carbon deposits, resulting in better performance.

LUBRICANTS

Your car has several different kinds of lubricants: engine oil, transmission fluid, power steering fluid, wheel bearing grease, and greases used in a lube job. Engine oil is so important that I will tell you about it in the next chapter. Transmission fluid and power steering fluid are checked each time the car is serviced, though you can check the level of these fluids yourself (see Chapter 17, Tips on Easy Tasks).

Repacking front wheel bearings involves putting a special kind of grease on the bearings. Greasing the car, having it lubricated, or having a lube job are terms that mean the same thing. A lube job refers to placing a special grease in the moving parts of the front suspension and steering mechanism. These parts move when the front wheels are steered from side to side and when they move up and down over bumps. A lube job also includes greasing certain joints on the drive shaft and checking the level of the lubricant in the differential. The drive shaft transmits power from the transmission to the rear wheels through the differential, which is composed of sets of gears in the rear axle. The differential enables the drive shaft to turn the rear axle shafts and also permits one axle shaft to go faster than the other when the car turns a curve. To repack the front wheels and grease your car, see Chapter 18, Tips on Medium Tasks.

If you neglect to have the proper lubricants used or replaced in your car at the correct intervals, you can expect costly repairs. Whether you do the lubricating tasks yourself or have the work done at a service station, it is your responsibility to keep records and see that a preventive maintenance program involving lubricants is carried out on your car.

10

Engine Oil

Oil prevents metal-to-metal contact of moving engine parts; it reduces friction and carries off heat, keeping the moving parts cooler. Oil helps maintain a seal for cylinders and protects against rust. Special additives in oil cut down on the build-up of acids that damage the engine.

VISCOSITY

Viscosity is the measure of oil thickness, *i.e.*, its rate of flow. The Society of Automotive Engineers (SAE) has developed a viscosity classification for oils: the higher the viscosity number, the heavier the oil. For example, SAE 30 is heavier than SAE 20. An oil with one number is a single viscosity oil. Multiple viscosity engine oils for all-season use are available; these have two or three numbers, for example, SAE 10W-30 or SAE 10W-20W-40. The letter W following the SAE number means it is a winter oil. Multiple viscosity oil will be correct for low-temperature starting and still meet high-temperature specifications.

QUESTION: What advantage does a single viscosity oil have over a multiple viscosity oil and vice versa? A single viscosity oil is especially good for high-horsepower, high-performance engines in an area of mild temperatures. A single viscosity oil at high outside temperatures will maintain more of its viscosity, or thickness, than the highest number of a multiple viscosity oil. For example, an SAE 30 oil will hold its viscosity better in hot summer temperatures than an SAE 10W-30 oil. The disadvantage of a single viscosity oil is that in cold weather, say 20° F., the engine is hard to turn over; if the battery is weak, you may not be able to crank the engine.

The advantage of a multiple viscosity engine oil, such as SAE 10W-30, is that in winter it behaves as a 10-viscosity oil, giving much easier starting. In summer or when the engine is hot, it behaves as a 30-viscosity oil, giving adequate protection to small- and medium-sized engines.

SERVICE REQUIREMENTS

The American Petroleum Institute (API) classified oil several years ago according to the quality required by the car. For example, SC classification met the warranty requirements in 1964, SD fulfilled warranty needs in 1968, and SE is the quality required for new-car warranty protection from 1972 models onward. Each can of oil is labeled with the quality, and I recommend that you buy only oil of SE quality. The more expensive name brands of oil contain additives that fully justify their higher price.

DANGER OF CHANGING OIL QUALITY

If you change from an SE oil to one that is not labeled SE, your car may consume more oil and build up sludge in its engine, which may cause problems such as overheating. If you buy a used car, you probably will not know what quality or viscosity of oil has been used in it. In that case, select a well-known brand of SE quality oil and use it continuously as you would in a new car.

Whatever brand of oil you use, keep a spare quart and a pouring spout in the trunk of your car; then you will have it in case of an emergency.

DETERGENT OILS

All automobile engine oils with an SE quality designation contain some additives, and one of these additives is a detergent. A detergent in oil acts like a detergent in your laundry: the laundry detergent cleans the clothes, and the engine oil detergent cleans the engine. A clean engine that has no excessive sludge, carbon, or other build-ups is a better-performing engine, and it will give more trouble-free miles and require less repair.

OIL WARNING LIGHT

Oil is forced under pressure by the oil pump to all parts of the engine. When the oil warning light on the dashboard comes on, stop the engine immediately! The light indicates that the oil pressure is low. Whatever the reason, the engine must be stopped at once to avoid damage. As a matter of fact, the engine may already be damaged when the idiot light comes on. Some older cars have an indicator gauge showing oil pressure. If the pressure is low, you can stop the engine and investigate and correct the trouble before damage occurs.

COLD CLIMATES

If you live in the northern states, where temperatures in winter frequently go below 0° F., you need special information about oils (see Chapter 19, Hints for Cold Climates).

SUMMARY

Do not mix or change quality of oil in your engine. Stick to the manufacturer's recommendations in the Owner's Manual. When you must add oil between changes, use oil of the same quality and viscosity that was put in when the oil was last changed.

QUESTION: Will my engine be damaged if I change brands of oil? No, as long as you buy an SE grade of a well-known brand your engine is well protected.

QUESTION: Does oil wear out? All engine oils contain additives that do beneficial things for the engine, such as reduce friction, reduce acids, suspend contaminants, and protect parts against unnecessary wear. These additives are slowly depleted in performing their jobs; if oil is used for a long period without being changed it will no longer accomplish its purpose. Oil becomes contaminated with water, metal particles, carbon, and other foreign matter. Though a filter helps remove foreign matter, none is 100 percent perfect. For these reasons, oil and oil filters should be changed at recommended intervals.

11

Tires

Deciding that you need to buy tires is fairly simple. Making the correct decision on the right kind of tire for your vehicle, for your kind of driving, and for your pocketbook is not easy for many drivers. Make this simple test to see if your tire tread is too thin. Take a Lincoln-head penny and place the top of Lincoln's head at the bottom of the shallowest tread groove. If you can see all of Lincoln's head, the tread is too worn and it is time to buy a new tire. Some buyers make a blind selection because of a sale, or listen to a glib salesman who may or may not be giving unbiased information. The following information should help you select the tires that will be best for your car.

Remember that your safety depends on the selection, use, and care of your tires. Buy the tires that fit your car, the load to be carried by the car, your type of driving, your roads, and your pocketbook. Incidentally, American tire manufacturers have tires that will fit most foreign cars.

Automobile tires may be grouped as conventional (nonradial) tires and radial tires.

CONVENTIONAL TIRES

The two kinds of conventional tires are the bias-ply tire (commonly called the bias tire) and the belted bias tire (commonly called the belted tire).

The bias tire has been on the market since about 1920. Cords are woven into layers, and each layer of cord is called a ply. The layers cross over one another at an angle to form the body of the tire. Plies

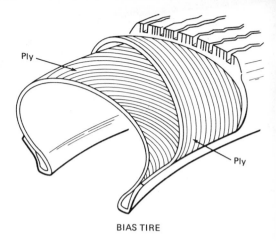

Bias tire, cutaway view

BIAS TIRE

always come in even numbers—two-ply, four-ply, or six-ply—and are usually made of polyester. The more plies, the stronger the tire.

Bias tires are rigid in tread and sidewall, and "squirm" more than other types. Squirming is the tire experts' term for the tread distortion that decreases traction and increases wear as the tire makes contact with the road. Bias tires tend to run hotter than other tires; and heat will shorten tire life. These tires usually are less expensive than belted or radial tires, and sales that advertise new tires at a surprisingly low price are probably for bias tires. The bias tire probably will be satisfactory if a car is driven at slow speeds around town, with little or no highway driving, but I do not recommend them for constant highway driving. Your neck and the lives of your passengers deserve a better, safer tire.

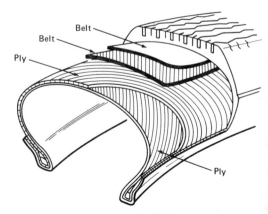

Belted tire, cutaway view

BELTED TIRE

The belted tire has been available for about forty years. The body of a belted tire is constructed much like the bias tire, with crisscrossed layers or plies of overlapping polyester cord. The big difference in this tire is the two or more additional belts, bands, or layers of material that go around the tire under the tread. These belts are made of fiberglass, rayon, or nylon.

The belted tire squirms less than the bias tire, runs cooler, and gives more mileage, so that its cost ultimately may be less per mile than that of a bias tire, even though a belted tire costs more initially. This is a much safer tire, and I recommend it over a bias tire.

RADIAL TIRES

Radial tires are the newest kind available. They were first manufactured and used successfully in other countries before appearing in the U.S., and have been available here for about twenty years.

The radial tire has one, two, or three plies, with the body cords running at right angles to the center line of the tire tread. All radial tires are belted with up to four plies underneath the tread. Radial body cords offer a choice of materials: polyester, rayon, and nylon. Belts may be made of steel or fiberglass.

Radial construction creates a flexible sidewall, and the tires appear to be in need of air even when properly inflated. This characteristic makes it even more important to have your own tire gauge and to check the tire pressure at regular intervals. Ask the tire dealer for the proper inflation pressures.

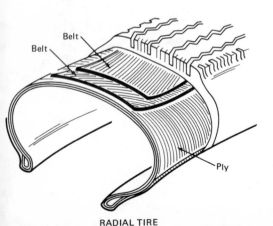

Belt

Belt

Ply

Radial tire, cutaway view

RADIAL TIRE

Radials run cooler, give the longest mileage (some radial tires are guaranteed by the manufacturer for 40,000 miles), are the safest, and cost the most of any tire available. Radial tires squirm less, and keep more tread on the road because of their belts and because they flex without heat build-up. This provides better traction, superior handling, and stability in turns. Most reports state that radials also give better gas mileage; about 7 percent better mileage is the national average for cars.

If you prefer radials on a new car that does not have them, consult with the dealer about swapping the tires before you drive the car. If you are now using bias or belted tires and would like to change to radials as your tires wear out—which I recommend for sustained highway driving and greatest tire dependability—there is one serious problem: you will have to buy five radial tires and have them installed all at once (your spare has to be a radial, too). *Do not mix* radial tires and conventional tires on your car! To do so is courting disaster as the car will sway easily, and steering can be difficult and dangerous. Before installing radials, check with the tire dealer to learn whether a special front-end alignment is required. All newly installed tires must be balanced. A dealer normally charges separately for balancing and does not include this in the price of the tire. Radials usually make a little more noise than conventional tires—another factor to consider before switching to radials.

ROTATION OF TIRES

All tires on a car do not wear at the same rate, and rotation usually helps to get maximum tire mileage. Bias and belted tires should be rotated about every 5,000 to 8,000 miles if you do the rotation yourself. One rotation plan is: spare to left front, left front to right rear, right rear to right front, right front to left rear, and left rear to spare. This is "crisscross" rotation. Some tire authorities now suggest that if you have to pay for having your tires rotated you should leave them in the same location up to 20,000 miles, unless one or more tires show unusual wear. Otherwise, the cost of rotation negates anything you have saved by having your tires rotated.

Do not crisscross radial tires. Always keep them on the same side of the car to avoid unnecessary stress on the tire. Some owners rotate radial tires to get more mileage. This is a good thing to do about every 5,000 to 8,000 miles if you rotate the tires yourself. Otherwise leave the

TIRE ROTATION

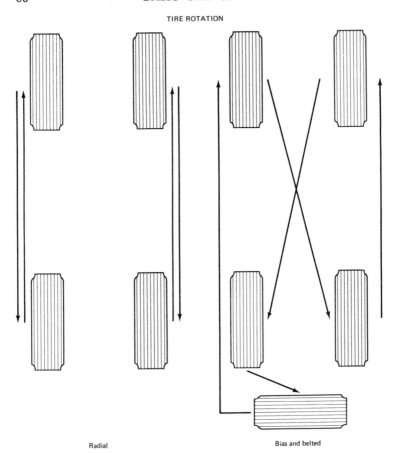

Radial   Bias and belted

Tire rotation

tires in their present positions up to 20,000 miles unless unusual wear develops. Here is a tire rotation plan for radials: right front to right rear, right rear to right front, left front to left rear, and left rear to left front. Note that the spare does not enter into this switch. Sooner or later one of the four tires will wear and need replacing, and you can install your spare and keep the worn tire as a spare for emergency purposes.

SPECIAL TIRES

Various types of blowout- and puncture-resistant tires are on the market. Some have a steel safety belt under the tread; others have an inner tire separated from the main body by an air space; in some a sealant is used to prevent air from escaping if a puncture should occur. Some of these tires have excessive heat build-up, and others are difficult to balance. Snow tires are available for drivers who live in colder climates (see Chapter 19, Hints for Cold Climates).

A new radial tire manufactured in the U.S. has recently appeared on the market. It is steel-belted like many other radials, but in addition has steel in the sidewalls. This tire is guaranteed for 50,000 miles. The manufacturer approves crisscross rotating this tire at intervals, as is done to a bias or belted tire.

Today's trend is toward low, wide-profile tires. Wide tires provide better road contact and better cornering, but drivers of some cars without power steering report that turning is harder with wide tires. On older cars wide-profile tires may not fit the rims and may rub the fender wells during turns. Be sure to check these points before changing the type of tire on your car. Consult your Owner's Manual and follow the manufacturer's recommendations.

TIRE QUALITY

At present no reliable rating system indicates the comparative quality of tires. There are no industry-wide, government, or other uniform systems of quality grades or standards. For example, "premium," "super," "first line," and "100 level" are brand grades or advertising terms and are not consistent from one brand to the next. Reports from unbiased tests, such as are found in *Consumer Reports,* are probably your best guides in selecting a quality tire.

All tires display certain kinds of information molded into the sidewalls: size and load capacity, maximum pressure in pounds per square inch (psi), brand name, cord composition, and the number of plies for both sidewall and tread. The Department of Transportation (DOT) label indicates the tire meets federal motor vehicle safety standards.

Size and load labeling of tires changed to a letter and numbering system several years ago. Charts are available at the tire dealer's store to show you what the other letters and numerals on your tire mean. An example is F78-14. The first letter gives the tire load capability. The F designation means the tire will support 1,280 pounds of weight when inflated to 24 psi. A tire labeled N would support 1,880 pounds of weight. The 78 means the tire profile height is 78 percent of the tire width. The 14 indicates a 14-inch rim. If R follows the first letter, for example ER78-14, the R says it is a radial tire.

Do not be too concerned about all the letters and numbers on your tire, as your dealer will help you select the right size and load limit. Two important things to remember are: do not buy tires smaller than your car's original equipment, and do not overinflate your tires. The maximum pressure is shown on the tire, for example, "max inflation 32 psi."

TIRE PRESSURE

If the maximum pressure indicated on the side of the tire is 32 psi, put slightly less than the maximum—say 28 to 30 psi—in your tires. Owner's Manuals usually recommend a tire pressure that is too low, sometimes as low as 24 psi. Remember the manufacturer of your car wants you to have a soft, easy, enjoyable ride, and he is not too concerned with the life of your tires. Reputable tire dealers will confirm these facts.

You should have your own tire gauge. To get an accurate reading, take the tire pressure when the tire is cold or has not been driven over one mile—the pressure inflates when the car is being driven (see Chapter 12, Four Regular Checks).

TIRE CARE

If tires wear equally on both edges but not in the center, they need additional air pressure. On the other hand, the air pressure is too high if tires show wear in the center. If the front tires wear on one edge more than on the other, a problem of alignment or worn front-end parts exists. Have the alignment checked by a shop that specializes in this job.

Most drivers know that a new tire should be balanced in order to give a smooth ride and longer tire wear. What some drivers do not realize is that a new tire must be round within allowable limits, or else the tire will cause excessive vibration, and no amount of balancing is going to cure the vibration. Practically all tire manufacturers today produce some tires that are not perfectly round. Do not condemn all tires of a particular brand because you get one tire that is out of round. If your new tire still has excessive vibration even though balanced, go back to your tire dealer and discuss the problem. A reputable dealer will usually have equipment to check the tire and the wheel and see if they are as round as they should be. If the tire is not round, he should "true" the tire or give you a financial adjustment on a new tire. Let me stress again the importance of buying a well-known brand of tire from a reputable dealer.

Trueing a tire consists of mounting the tire on a special machine that rotates the tire slowly while a sharp edge removes excess rubber until the tire is round within allowable tolerances. A small town may not have a shop that trues tires, but most cities have shops that offer this service.

Always keep a valve cap on the threaded valve stem of each tire to keep out sand, dust, and other foreign matter. A valve stem extension may be needed if the rims are fitted with covers. The extension seals the end of the valve stem and takes the place of a valve cap.

To get the longest wear from your tires, keep them inflated to the pressure I have recommended, have the tires balanced and trued if necessary, keep your front end aligned, and drive responsibly with no "burning rubber" when you start and no sliding when you stop. And *never* drive on a flat tire.

FRONT-END ALIGNMENT

For long tire life the front end of your car should be properly aligned. Rear wheels do not need aligning on American cars; they will be aligned correctly unless a mechanical defect exists, such as a bent rear axle. (Some foreign cars should have the rear wheel alignment checked and corrected as well as the front wheel alignment.) When you put new tires on the front wheels, take the car to a reputable shop that aligns front ends and have the alignment checked. Usually the shop will not charge for this service, provided you agree to have any needed alignment work done at that shop. A reputable shop that aligns your front end cannot guarantee the alignment to last for a certain period of time or a certain number of miles driven. You might leave the shop and immediately strike a pothole or boulder in the road, or bump into a curb too hard and throw the front end out of alignment.

GUARANTEES

Most new tires carry some type of guarantee, either on time or mileage. Adjustments are made on a pro-rata share of the number of miles or months the tire has been driven. Guarantees differ, so it is important to understand clearly all conditions and terms. Most tires are guaranteed for the life of the original tread and against tire failures resulting from ordinary road hazards and defects in materials and workmanship. When you return a defective tire to a dealer for a financial adjustment, he measures the tread and determines the percentage of wear left in the tire. This percentage determines the amount of discount you receive on the cost of a new replacement tire. When tires have worn unevenly, the dealer makes the tread depth measurement where the greatest wear occurred.

You may void the guarantee by abusing the tire, such as driving on a flat. Proper tire pressure, proper balancing, and proper front-end alignment are also your responsibilities.

CHECKING THE TIRES

When you are making the four regular checks every two weeks or every 500 miles, examine the tires to see whether any unusual wear is occurring. Uneven tread wear may indicate the alignment should be checked. Indentions or pits around the tire may indicate worn shocks that need replacing. A shimmy at highway speeds usually indicates that the tires need balancing; if the car pulls to one side when you lift your hands off the wheel, alignment may be the problem. Trying to squeeze extra miles out of a badly worn tire can be dangerous and is false economy. Some states have periodic car inspections, and the tires are one of the things that are checked. About 90 percent of all flat tires occur after some part of the tire tread has worn to $\frac{1}{16}$-inch or less.

Shop around when your tires begin to show signs of wear and need replacing. Prices for a particular tire often vary from one dealer to another. Watch the advertisements for tire sales that may save additional money. Remember that the tire that costs the least is not necessarily the best bargain. Quality and tread life vary as do guarantees. Choose a dealer with a quality line of tires and a good reputation for service.

RECAPS AND RETREADS

Drivers who buy recaps and retreads are usually those who cannot afford new tires and who are willing to take the extra risk of tire failure. Some drivers use recaps and retreads successfully for slow, around-town driving. They are too dangerous for highway driving and carrying heavy loads. Your safest, most dependable choice is to buy new tires.

PUNCTURES

Tire punctures happen to practically all motorists at some time. See Chapter 17, Tips on Easy Tasks, to put on the spare tire. I suggest that you take the flat tire to a service station or tire dealer to have it repaired.

12

Four Regular Checks

Many drivers take their cars to a service station or garage for major tune-ups and repairs, as well as minor servicing such as lube jobs and changing the oil and oil filter. The length of time between these service procedures varies according to how much you drive, but you should make four regular checks yourself. (You will only have to make three regular checks if your car has an air-cooled engine.) About every two weeks or every 500 miles of driving, or just prior to a long trip, check the following:

1. Engine oil level
2. Liquid level in the battery
3. Air pressure in the tires
4. Liquid level in the radiator (skip this check if you have an air-cooled engine)

ENGINE OIL LEVEL

Locate the oil dipstick, which is usually found on one side of the engine. Do not confuse the oil dipstick with the transmission fluid dipstick on a car that has automatic transmission. The transmission fluid dipstick is located at the rear of the engine near the fire wall.

The best time to check the engine oil level is before you drive the car, since you cannot make an accurate measurement immediately after the engine stops running; some of the oil is in the upper part of the engine, and it will take five or ten minutes for the oil to drain down so the reading will be accurate. The car *must* be on a level surface.

Grasp the oil dipstick by the loop of metal and pull it straight out, then use a cloth or a piece of paper to wipe it clean. You will find markings on the dipstick that read ADD (at the lower mark) and FULL (at the upper mark). After wiping, replace the dipstick in the sheath and insert it as far as possible.

Next pull the dipstick straight out, without any jiggling or back-and-forth movements. You will see a film of oil that indicates the level of oil in the engine. If the oil level on the dipstick is at the full mark or in between FULL and ADD, the engine has enough oil. When the oil level is at the add mark or lower, oil needs to be added. Normally one quart will bring the level to the full mark. You will need one or more quart cans of the proper oil and a pouring spout, available at auto parts stores. Insert the back end of the pouring spout in the can, applying force to puncture the can. If you do not have a pouring spout, you can use a beer can opener and a funnel to achieve the same results.

Now locate the oil filler cap, which is somewhere on the top or side of the engine. Often this cap will have the word "oil" stamped on top. You may have to turn the cap counterclockwise and then lift to remove it, though on some cars the oil filler cap pulls straight out. Now use the pouring spout or funnel and add a quart of oil to the engine. Keep a rag handy to wipe up any spills. Wait five minutes and then check the oil again to be sure it is at the proper level. It may take two quarts of oil to bring the level to the full mark.

Now a word of caution. If you are starting on a long trip and you find upon checking the oil that the level is slightly above the add mark, go ahead and put in a quart of oil. No damage will be done if the level goes slightly above full; the engine will simply throw the oil out. The oil level at full gives maximum protection for long trips.

All engines burn or leak varying amounts of oil. As long as you do not have to add a quart more often than every 1,000 miles of driving, you need not be concerned. Do not forget to replace the oil filler cap after adding oil to the engine.

LIQUID LEVEL IN THE BATTERY

Most auto batteries have six vent caps, so you can add water as needed. The newest type of battery has no vent caps and never needs to have water added.

Maintain the proper level of liquid in the battery to avoid damage.

If the liquid around the plates is low, heat will cause the plates to warp, shortening the life of the battery. A battery with one or more dry cells or with liquid too low is not dependable and probably will not start your car.

Do not smoke or have a lighted flame near a battery when you check it, because of the danger of an explosion from the hydrogen gas given off by the battery.

Remove each of the six caps found on the top of a twelve-volt battery (the standard size in most cars), and be careful in handling the vent caps—they have acid on them which can damage your car's paint or your clothes, or cause a burn on your skin. Since each cell is insulated and separate from all the others, the fact that the liquid level is correct for the first cell does not mean it is correct in all the cells. The vent caps are not always easy to remove; grasp the cap firmly and exert pressure back and forth as you tug on it until the cap comes off. Put the caps where they cannot fall down into the engine compartment.

With the vent caps off, look into each cell to see if the liquid level is high enough. The surface of the liquid in the cell forms a split ring when the level is correct. Each battery manufacturer has designed this split-ring indicator in the cell so you can tell when the liquid is high enough.

Liquid level in battery

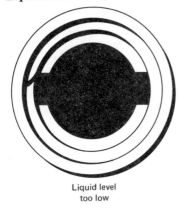

Liquid level
too low

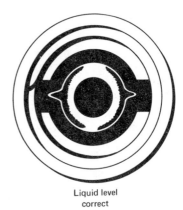

Liquid level
correct

If the liquid is low, add distilled water to achieve the proper level but do not fill the cell to the top. The battery gets warm during use, and if it is too full, the solution will run over, wasting acid and causing unnecessary corrosion on the metal battery connections and the metal battery case. Replace the caps, pushing them down firmly.

Distilled water is best for your battery, because it does not contain minerals. You can buy it, or you can get it free by collecting rainwater in a plastic or glass container, straining it through cheesecloth or a nylon stocking to remove dust, pollen, and other foreign matter. Do not catch the rainwater in a metal container; metal adds metallic ions that harm a battery.

Some older Delco batteries have a "Delco eye" that appears dark if the liquid level is adequate and lighter when the liquid is low. As the eye is located in only one cell cap, it is not dependable; each cell must be checked. The condition of one cell does not tell you anything about the condition of the other cells. Newer Delco batteries do not have this feature.

QUESTION: Why not use well water or tap water in my car battery? Any water other than distilled water probably contains iron, calcium, magnesium, or other minerals, which are harmful to batteries and shorten their lives.

QUESTION: Is boiled water the same as distilled water? No, boiling the water does not remove the minerals but only concentrates them; some water boils off, and the minerals remain in the container.

AIR PRESSURE IN THE TIRES

All tires lose pressure slowly. The tires are made of materials that allow molecules of air to pass through at a slow rate. Check the tires about every two weeks when you make the other regular checks, making sure to check the spare tire too. Check a bias or belted tire at once if it appears low; a leak may have developed in the tire or in the valve and it should be inspected at a service station. You cannot look at a radial tire and tell whether it needs air; radial tires always look low because of their shape.

Buy a pocket tire-pressure gauge that measures approximately 10 to 50 pounds from an auto parts supply store; it will probably be more accurate than the tire-pressure gauges used at many service stations. It is preferable to check your tires before the car has been driven over one mile, since driving causes the tires to warm up and increases the

Tire pressure gauge

air pressure. It is best to check the tires at a place where compressed air is available, so you can add air if it is needed, but if you have to drive more than a mile to get there, check the air pressure before you leave home and determine how many pounds of air you need. Check the pressure again at the station and add the needed pounds of air. For example, if your tire gauge reads 25 pounds at home, you need three pounds to bring it to 28. After driving to the station, add three pounds —whatever the pressure reads.

The top end of the tire gauge is fashioned at about a 45-degree angle to the body of the gauge. If the tire has a valve stem with a cap, remove the cap. Hold the gauge firmly in your hand with the round access top end positioned above the valve stem. Apply the end against the valve stem with a quick thrusting motion, which releases a small amount of air from the tire as the pressure is measured. The released air causes an indicator rod to move out of the shaft of the tire gauge. Do not continue to hold the gauge on the valve stem, or the gauge will release too much air. Press the gauge down quickly and then let up. The indicator rod is marked with numbers, usually in fives, and has marks in between indicating one-pound increments. Read the gauge by noting the last visible number on the indicator rod, for example, 28, 29, or 30 (pounds).

Add the correct pressure that you need for your tires by applying the nozzle of the compressed-air hose flat against the valve stem. (See Chapter 11, Tires, for information about the proper air pressure for your tires.) Most machines at service stations have a meter that you can set to ring when the proper pressure is reached. Otherwise, add needed air with a one-second or two-second input, and use your gauge to measure the pressure between each application of air. A little practice makes perfect. Remember to replace the valve stem cap.

LIQUID LEVEL IN THE RADIATOR

It is important to keep the proper liquid level in the radiator. Your car has a conventional cooling system or a closed cooling system. Newer cars often have a closed cooling system that is easy to identify and to check; a translucent plastic container mounted near the front of the engine has a hose that leads from the container to the top of the radiator near the cap. As the liquid gets hot in the radiator and expands, it flows into the plastic container. Conversely, as the radiator cools liquid is drawn back into the radiator. Check the level of the coolant when the engine is cold.

The radiator cap on a closed cooling system is labeled "Do Not Open." Normally you should follow this instruction, and add any needed coolant to the plastic container. Markings on the side of the plastic container read FULL HOT and FULL COLD, which are the minimum amounts of coolant needed. If the coolant level is below the full-cold mark, open the lid of the plastic container and add the proper coolant (see Chapter 7, The Cooling System) to bring the level up to halfway between the full-cold and full-hot markings. This extra amount of coolant simply gives you a safety factor against the coolant getting too low and the engine overheating.

Your American car probably has a conventional cooling system if it is older than 1972. On such a car the radiator cap must be removed to check the level of the coolant. Never remove the radiator cap when the engine is hot. To do so will waste coolant, and you may be *scalded*. To open the radiator cap, you must grasp it firmly and depress hard while you turn the cap counterclockwise. Radiator caps are made hard to open purposely, so they make a good seal and do not vibrate, become loose, and then fall off. Some radiator caps have a small lever

Coolant reserve container

marked "pressure removal" or something similar to permit you to release the pressure; this should be done before you open the radiator cap. You have to loosen some caps one-fourth turn to release the pressure. Even though you think the engine has cooled, place a heavy cloth over the cap before opening it.

The liquid in the radiator should be visible, covering the radiator core, which can be seen approximately 2 to 3 inches below the cap. Add the proper coolant (see Chapter 7, The Cooling System) to the radiator if the liquid is low. Do not fill the radiator completely to the top. Coolant expands when it gets hot, and a full radiator will overflow.

Replace the radiator cap after checking the liquid. Turn the cap forcibly in a clockwise direction until it is properly closed. Coolant will be wasted if you do not put the cap on tightly. All cooling systems are under pressure. The radiator cap must maintain the proper pressure, or it will have to be replaced.

Caution! If you need to add coolant to the radiator of a hot engine in an emergency, crank the engine and let it idle as you add the coolant. Otherwise you may seriously damage the engine.

13

Common Problems

Various problems plague drivers at one time or another. In this chapter I have selected a few common problems that affect many people throughout the country.

COST OF OPERATION

The most common problem that concerns practically all drivers is the high cost of operation—often resulting from high fuel consumption—compounded in recent years by huge increases in the cost of gasoline. Most authorities say we can expect higher prices for gas in the future, so what reasonable steps can be taken to cut operating costs?

Let's analyze six areas that have the greatest effect on your driving expenses: car selection and options, car maintenance, tune-ups, driving techniques, personal habits, and insurance.

Car Selection and Options

If your car is relatively new and you plan to keep it a long time, you will have to live with your selection and most of the options. If you are planning to buy a car, take time to study different sizes, makes, and features, and buy a car that will meet your needs yet give you satisfactory mileage.

A law of physics states that the more pounds to be moved at a given speed the more energy (gasoline) will be required. Generally, the lighter the car (compact or subcompact size) the more miles per gallon you can expect. Nevertheless, safety may be more important to you than extra gas mileage, and the heavier the car the safer you are, especially at high speeds. Another consideration in favor of larger cars is the possibility of using the car in a car pool.

A car with manual transmission gets better gas mileage than the same car with automatic transmission. Shifting gears for yourself with manual transmission may give you up to 15 percent better gas mileage.

An air conditioner on your car will cut your gas mileage about one to three miles to the gallon, so use your air conditioner only when you absolutely need it, keeping in mind that it is costing you money. *Caution!* Run your air conditioner at least fifteen minutes a week, all year round. Running it circulates the oil, which keeps the seal on the shaft lubricated. A dry seal permits freon gas to escape, which can require servicing or repair.

Radial tires give slightly better gas mileage than other tires, but do not rush down to swap your perfectly good bias or belted tires for radials, as the improvement is minor (about 7 percent for most cars).

Car Maintenance

Better gas mileage is a fringe benefit of proper maintenance. Having the engine tuned at regular intervals will directly improve your gas mileage. Changing your dirty air cleaner will also improve gas mileage, since a dirty air cleaner restricts the air flow to the carburetor, causing more gas to be drawn to the carburetor. The engine then has a richer mixture than normal, which wastes gas.

The cooling system thermostat influences gas consumption. The thermostat should cause the engine to warm up quickly enough so that the heater gives off hot air after about five minutes in cold weather. Your engine will be slow to warm up if your thermostat is defective. While cold, the engine runs inefficiently, wasting gas. An engine at the proper operating temperature gives the best gas mileage, other factors being equal. Replace a defective thermostat at once with a new one designed for your car. To do this job yourself, see Chapter 18, Tips on Medium Tasks.

A dirty or faulty carburetor or a sticking automatic choke wastes gas and contributes to air pollution. A good mechanic will check these areas and correct any trouble when your car is tuned.

Underinflated tires cause increased fuel consumption and greater tire wear. Five pounds of underinflation can waste a half-gallon or more of gasoline out of every tankful.

Tune-ups

To get the best gas mileage, a tune-up is necessary periodically; it does not come under the warranty requirements. A tune-up usually includes: replacing the plugs, points, and condenser; adjusting the carburetor; checking and adjusting the timing; and inspecting the distributor cap, the rotor button, and the electrical wiring. How often a tune-up is needed varies with different makes and ages of cars and the driving conditions (stop-and-go driving, short trips, long trips, and high speed), but generally a car should have a tune-up approximately every 10,000 miles. Poor gas mileage, hard starting, and sluggish pickup are indications tht you need a tune-up. When these conditions occur, have your car tuned to avoid a possible breakdown.

Tuning a car is not a job for the average driver. A person needs considerable experience and knowledge as a mechanic and must be familiar with a particular car to tune it properly. Antipollution equipment installed on newer cars presents additional complications for tuning an engine. A mechanic who tunes your car has a considerable investment in the proper equipment, which includes: technical manuals, a dwell meter, a feeler gauge for setting points, a timing light, a compression gauge, wrenches, and other tools.

Driving Techniques

Most experienced drivers resent being told how to drive. This section is only for those drivers who want to improve their gas mileage and who are willing to consider changes in their driving techniques to accomplish this goal.

The most rewarding change you can make is to drive slower. A highway speed of 50 mph yields up to four miles per gallon more than a speed of 70 mph; obviously, driving slower will conserve fuel. The national speed limit of 55 mph is designed to save fuel.

Try to maintain a steady speed, as braking and accelerating use more gas. You can also conserve fuel by anticipating signal light changes and slowing down to avoid a complete stop. Riding the brake makes your engine work harder, uses up more gas, and wears out the brake linings or pads.

Avoid jackrabbit starts. Every time you step on the accelerator a spurt of gas goes into the carburetor. Sudden spurts waste gas, since not all of it can be burned efficiently in the engine. "Scratching off" or "burning rubber" may be a teen-ager's way of getting attention, but it wastes fuel and causes unnecessary wear on tires and other component parts of the auto.

Avoid long warm-ups. When the engine is first cranked, allow it to idle only long enough to ensure a satisfactory performance when you drive away. Racing the engine immediately after starting wastes gas and causes excessive wear on the engine. Turn the engine off when you are parked for more than a minute or two; idling gives you zero miles per gallon.

Buy the grade of gas recommended by your Owner's Manual: unleaded, regular, or premium. If your car calls for unleaded gasoline, be certain to use *only* that; otherwise serious trouble will result. If your car is designed for regular gas, you are wasting money to burn premium fuel all the time. Large American cars manufactured before 1975 often need premium gas. Use only premium gasoline in such a car, because regular will probably cause "pinging" when you accelerate. This high-pitched noise indicates the fuel is burning prematurely, which wastes gas and can be harmful to the engine.

Personal Habits

Personal habits are hard to change, and you can do so only if you have a strong desire to cut driving costs. Here are some suggestions— perhaps you can think of other things that you and your family can do.

To save money on driving, simply drive fewer miles. You probably feel it does not take very much gas to go short distances, but reports show that one-half of all the fuel used in passenger cars is consumed in trips of three miles or less. Buy your gas at cut-rate stations, preferably the self-service kind. Cut-rate, unknown gas brands are usually just as high quality as well-known brands, and frequently it is the same gas from the same source. Drive your car more years before you trade or sell it; the depreciation cost is greatest in the early years of a car's life.

Insurance

Review your car insurance; you may not really need collision insurance if your car is four years old or older. If you have adequate hospital and medical insurance, you may not need medical coverage in your automobile insurance policy. (Do not confuse the above insurance with liability insurance, which every driver needs and which is required by many states.)

LIMITED LOCAL CAR USE AND SLOW DRIVING

Short trips, stop-and-go driving, and slow speeds are hard on a car. You use the brakes more frequently in driving around town than on longer trips. On short trips the exhaust system does not get hot enough to evaporate the moisture that has condensed in the muffler and tail-pipe, and because moisture causes rust, it will shorten the life of these parts.

Slow driving tends to increase the carbon build-up in the engine, particularly if you use regular leaded gasoline. Carbon build-up causes poor engine performance, such as less pickup and difficulty in starting the car. If you normally burn regular leaded gas, try using premium fuel about every fourth or fifth tank. Then take your car on the high-way and drive five or ten miles at the legal limit. Premium gasoline will help burn out the excess carbon and should improve engine per-formance.

Your tires may rot out before they wear out. After five years, the rubber valve stem may rot; one indication is that your tires keep losing air pressure. A service station can replace the valve stem at low cost.

It is important to stress that *time* as well as *miles driven* determine the frequency of service procedures such as lube jobs, oil and filter changes, and tune-ups. It is *your* responsibility to tell your mechanic when you want service done.

Every engine should be run at a medium-fast rate for ten to fifteen minutes each week. Doing this will keep the battery charged and ready to start the car. Do not just start the car and let the engine idle; keep the accelerator depressed slightly. It is important to run the air conditioner and the engine each week; do this yourself if your car is not driven for a week, or arrange for someone else to do it.

WINDSHIELD WIPERS

Many drivers overlook or postpone one area of preventive main-tenance more than any other—the maintenance or replacement of windshield wiper blades. The rubber blades deteriorate from age, sun-light, and the road oil that gets on them by splashing on the wind-shield. As blades get older, the rubber cracks or hardens and fails to do its job. When you notice your wipers are not cleaning the windshield as they should, it is time to correct the trouble. Do not postpone it. Another sign that blades need replacing is when the rubber splits and tears. Make sure you replace both wiper blades at the same time; if one wiper is worn out, the other one is about to go too.

Here are some visible or audible indicators that the wipers need attention:

1. Streaking—the blade leaves untouched moisture within its wiping arc.
2. Hazing—a thin film covers all or most of the wiping area even after you wipe the blade with a clean cloth. Try cleaning the inside of your window before replacing blades; tobacco smoke, in particular, will haze the inside of the windshield.
3. Chattering—a peculiar, intermittent, stuttering noise and a vibrating motion accompany the blade as it goes back and forth.
4. Rattling—the wiper blades give out a rattling noise, which sounds like the blade is loose.

Some drivers have new blades installed at the service station or garage. You can do this job yourself and save money (see Chapter 17, Tips on Easy Tasks).

All modern cars have an electric windshield washer device. A translucent plastic container under the hood holds the solution that is sprayed on the windshield. When your windshield washer stops working, the liquid is probably used up. Simply remove the top of the plastic container and refill with water or water and cleaning chemicals, such as Windex, or a preparation made for this purpose. Do not confuse this container with the coolant reserve container, which is clearly connected to the radiator by a hose.

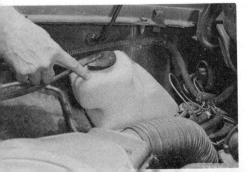

Windshield washer reservoir

If the supply container has plenty of liquid and the windshield washer still will not work, the most likely trouble is a stopped-up filter screen on the end of the hose connected to the container. Remove the filter screen and try the windshield washer; if it now works, then the filter screen is causing the trouble. Put it in a cup containing vinegar to soak overnight. If this does not dissolve the calcium and magnesium deposits that came from the water, you may have to buy a new filter screen from your auto parts store or the parts department of your car dealer.

The windshield washer, especially on an older car, still may not work after you try these troubleshooting techniques. The electric pump that powers the washer to spray liquid on the windshield may be worn out. If so, you can either buy a kit at an auto parts store or have a garage replace the pump. The kit consists of a replacement pump and hoses, which you can install with a few small hand tools.

DIESELING

This word means that an engine continues to run after you turn off the ignition; the condition may result from several causes. The spark timing may not be set properly or there may be an excessive amount of carbon build-up in the engine from slow, stop-and-go driving. Antipollution devices can also contribute to this problem. You may eliminate dieseling by having the timing set properly. Fill the tank with premium gas occasionally and drive at the legal highway speed for five or ten miles to help burn off the excess carbon in the engine. If the problem persists, you can stop dieseling by simply turning the engine off while the car is in gear.

INSECTS

In some areas of the country, insects create problems by accumulating in large numbers on the radiator, obstructing the flow of air and causing the engine to overheat. The best solution is to install a screen made of plastic net or other material that allows the air to pass through easily. Mount the screen on the front of the car to prevent the radiator from clogging and to protect the painted surface behind the screen.

Some insects, such as the love bug, can be harmful to the painted surface of the car. Acid in the bodies of the insects damages the paint if the bodies are left on the surface for more than a day. Wash all the insects off painted surfaces at least once a day. An occasional heavy application of paste wax will help protect the paint. You can also apply one of the supermarket products that help prevent sticking (Pam or Cooking Ease) to make it easier to wash off the insects. Reapply the protective material after washing the car.

14

Troubleshooting

Does your car go clang, clang, clang or chug, chug, snort instead of whirr-purr? Something is wrong. A trained, experienced mechanic can tell a lot about an engine just by listening to it run. A crude comparison is the physician who uses a stethoscope to listen to your breathing and heartbeat. You, the amateur do-it-yourselfer, cannot possibly become an expert at diagnosing the multitude of things that could be ailing your car by reading books.

In this chapter, we will look at a few common symptoms and discuss what they might mean and what you can do. You may need a helper and a few basic tools to correct some of the troubles.

THE ENGINE WILL NOT START

The battery has plenty of power to spin the engine, and the gas gauge indicates at least a quarter tank of fuel. The engine has been running recently, but now it will not crank. Either an electrical problem or an impedance in the flow of gas to the carburetor is the likely cause; two tests will help you to determine the cause. Make the electric test first for safety reasons.

To make a simple electric test, locate the wire in the center of the distributor. (The distributor is the round, octopuslike device with wires leading to each spark plug.) Grasp the center wire firmly and pull straight up. Hold the wire you remove about ⅛-inch from a metal part of the engine. Get a helper to turn the ignition key to turn the engine over several times. The electrical system is probably all right if a spark is produced by the distributor wire.

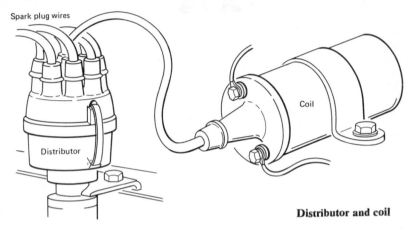

Spark plug wires

Coil

Distributor

Distributor and coil

Suppose you do not see any spark when you hold the wire from the distributor to within ⅛-inch of the metal engine. The other end of the wire in your hand goes to the top of the coil. (The coil resembles a metal can about 2½ inches in diameter and about 5 inches high.) Push this end of the wire firmly into the receptacle on top of the coil. Then try the spark test again. If there is still no spark between the wire from the distributor and the engine, the problem is in the electrical system and could be one of many things, most of which you probably cannot repair: coil, condenser, points, rotor button.

Another possible problem you can fix is when a wire inside the distributor is shorted against the metal side of the distributor. This happened to me. I was driving along when the engine suddenly stopped, just as though the ignition switch had been turned off. Another person and I made the simple spark test, and I saw no spark. I took a screwdriver and turned the holding screws on the side of the distributor one-half turn counterclockwise so I could remove the distributor lid. Then I noticed a wire with a bare spot, touching the inner side of the distributor. This bare wire shorted out the electrical system. I wrapped plastic electrician's tape around the wire, covering the bare place to prevent shorting. I replaced the lid on the distributor and turned the holding screws clockwise to fasten the lid securely. Then I replaced the wire in the center of the distributor, started the car easily, and was on my way. The wire that shorted was replaced later with a new wire.

To make a fuel test, open the hood and remove the air cleaner in order to look in the top of the carburetor. Ask a helper to pump the accelerator two or three times. You should see gas being pumped into the engine, or a white vapor coming out of the top of the carburetor. You may smell a strong odor of gasoline. Sometimes you can hear a slight hissing noise caused by the gas being sprayed through the jet as the accelerator is moved up and down. *Do not smoke* or have a flame of any kind near the engine while doing this test! In vapor form gas ignites easily. If you see no gas and your tank is at least one-fourth full, something is stopping the flow of gas between the tank and the carburetor. You need the help of a mechanic.

If the gas is flowing, but the engine still will not start, it may be flooded. Let the engine sit for five minutes, then depress the accelerator, holding it down to the floor. Try cranking the engine two or three times, giving it five-second bursts of rotation. If the engine does not start, wait another five minutes, and try again.

THE ENGINE SKIPS

If the engine skips when you stop for a traffic light but seems to run smoothly at 40 to 50 mph, you may have one or more defective spark plugs. Make this simple test for a defective spark plug. Start the engine, open the hood, and use gloves to carefully remove the wire from each plug, one at a time. Pull the spark plug boot, not the wire. The boot is a rubber cover that fits over the plug.

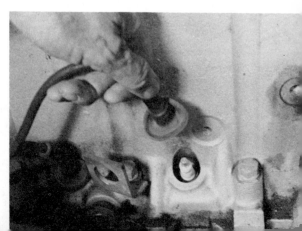

Spark plug boot

Listen to the effect on the engine as each wire is removed; then replace the wire. Removing each wire should have the effect of slowing the engine and causing it to skip worse. Removing a wire with no effect indicates the source of the trouble. Have a plug installed at that location; the new plug should have the numerical designation given in the Owner's Manual or an equivalent number in another reputable brand. Information on how to change spark plugs is not given in this book because the spark plugs are usually changed when a mechanic tunes the engine. Whether you can change one faulty plug depends on the engine and the difficulty of getting to that particular plug, the tools you have, and your mechanical ability, though it is a relatively simple task. If the engine idles smoothly after the new plug is installed, the trouble was a faulty plug. If that does not help, it is time for a mechanic.

TOWING TIPS

Your car with automatic transmission will not run, and you need a mechanic. You have a second vehicle or a friend who offers to tow your car to the shop to save the towing fee. *Do not do this!* Towing a car with automatic transmission, even in neutral, will damage the transmission of many cars and cause expensive repairs. Your Owner's Manual will tell you if your car can be towed without damaging the automatic transmission. The drive shaft can be disconnected so the transmission will not be damaged, but that is a job for a mechanic, not an amateur. A tow truck operator will lift the rear of the car to save the transmission. Another reason for not towing your car with another car is that you may be breaking the law in some municipalities. If your car has manual transmission, you may tow it without damaging the transmission, but be careful. Towing is risky, as you may damage one or both cars if they collide.

AIR CONDITIONER AND HEATER PROBLEMS

If the fan that blows cold air from the air conditioner or hot air from the heater stops, first check the fuse block for a blown fuse. You can have a blown fuse replaced or do it yourself (see Chapter 17, Tips on Easy Tasks). If the fan works when you turn the air conditioner on but the air that is blown out is not cold, turn off the engine, open the hood, and examine the belt that drives the air conditioner compressor. Have a loose belt tightened or a broken or frayed belt replaced; you can also do this task yourself (see Chapter 18, Tips on Medium Tasks). Go to an air conditioner repair shop if the drive belt is not the problem.

A car air conditioner sometimes cools perfectly for thirty minutes or an hour. Then the air flow decreases and the cooling stops. Try turning the air conditioner off for twenty or thirty minutes. It may work perfectly for a time and then stop cooling again. An explanation is that the cooling coil is building up a layer of ice, which effectively blocks the air flow and the cooling power. Turning the air conditioner off for a period of time allows the ice to melt, and the air conditioner again will work perfectly for a while. The trouble will not get any better, so take the car to an air conditioner repair shop.

Do not forget to operate your air conditioner at least ten to fifteen minutes a week all year round, even during winter months.

TIRE VIBRATION

What can you do if you feel vibration as you drive down the road? First, try the car on a smooth road, because the trouble may be caused by road conditions. If you just bought new tires, one or more may need to be balanced or trued (see Chapter 11, Tires). If you have had the tires several months and the vibration has just started, one or more weights may have fallen off the wheel(s), and you need to have the balancing checked. If the vibration shakes the steering wheel, the problem is probably a front wheel or the front end. Take the car to a reputable shop.

PULLING BRAKES

You are driving, apply the brakes, and the car pulls strongly to one side. What is the problem? Some water may be on your brakes if you have been driving in rain or on wet roads. Drive for about one-tenth of a mile with your left foot depressing the brake pedal slightly. The heat produced by friction should dry out the brakes. Then try stopping to see if the brakes still pull. Try this procedure once more if you notice an improvement. If there is no improvement and the brakes continue to pull to one side, you may need just a new brake pad, or you may have a more serious brake problem.

Never take chances with faulty brakes! See a mechanic at once if brakes make unusual noises, feel "spongy" when you push the foot pedal, pull to one side, or act up in other disconcerting ways. Brake repair is not a do-it-yourself job. You need a mechanic who is knowledgeable, experienced, and honest to do your brake repairs.

SLUGGISH STARTER

Which is the culprit if the starter just barely turns the engine over when you turn the ignition switch: starter, alternator, or battery? If the engine is cold, the battery is probably weak, which may be the result of a defective alternator. Have the battery checked where you purchased it or at a service station. If it is defective and still under warranty, the dealer will give you a financial adjustment. If all the cells are low and are not shorted, have the alternator checked. If the starter spins a cold engine but barely turns a hot engine, the trouble is probably a defective starter.

15

Accidents and Emergencies

ACCIDENTS

Each year many drivers are involved in accidents. The National Safety Council reports that 17,800,000 male drivers and 7,300,000 female drivers were involved in reportable accidents in a recent year. Though males are involved in more accidents than females, the difference is due in part to the amount of driving each sex does and the differences in the driving locations and conditions. For example, more men than women drive taxis and transfer trucks, which are considered more hazardous than ordinary driving around town.

To lessen your chances of having an accident, I recommend that you enroll in a DDC (defensive driving course), an eight-hour course designed for experienced drivers. The DDC teaches experienced drivers the types and causes of automobile accidents and how to prevent them. Practically all drivers fall into some dangerous driving habits, and this course will help you to identify these practices and correct them. Originated by the National Safety Council, it is available through local safety organizations and law enforcement agencies. The course is continually being upgraded and improved, and I believe accidents would substantially decrease if experienced drivers took it every five years.

If you are involved in an accident but are not seriously hurt, you should give first aid to anyone who may be injured, though you should not move an injured person unless absolutely necessary. Some states have passed a "Good Samaritan" law that protects you from being sued later if you give first aid to help the victim.

Keep cool! Turn on your emergency flashers or activate emergency flares to decrease the chances of involving another vehicle; at night or in bad weather, this is a must. Send for the police, and do not move any vehicle until they arrive.

You should both obtain and render the following information for *each* vehicle involved in the accident, making sure to also list the names of the law officers present:

Driver's name ———————————————————————

Driver's address ———————————————————————

Driver's phone number ————————————————————

Company carrying insurance ————————————————

Insurance policy number ——————————————————

License plate number ————————————————————

Make of vehicle ————————————————————————

Passenger(s) name(s) ————————————————————

Passenger(s) address(es) ——————————————————

GENERAL INFORMATION:

Names of law officers —————————————————————

Name(s) of any witness(es) ————————————————

Witness's address ————————————————————————

Witness's phone number ————————————————————

Make no agreements or settlements, but give the investigating officer complete details to the best of your knowledge and belief. Laws vary by states, and sometimes the courts will have to decide who or what caused the accident. Notify your insurance company as soon as possible after an accident.

EMERGENCIES

Every driver should expect emergencies and try to be prepared for them. It is impossible to list all driving emergencies, but here are a few examples to test your skills and reactions.

1. You are approaching a car that begins to veer over to your side of the road for no apparent reason. The driver may be asleep, drunk, ill, or not paying attention. What can you do? Slow down and pull as far as possible to the right-hand side of the road, while signaling with your lights and horn to warn the other driver of the danger. If there is a shoulder on your side of the road, do not hesitate to drive on it. Steer

into a ditch or any open ground on the right side that is free of obstructions if he continues toward you. Do not try to outguess him by steering to the left, since he may wake up or recover and swerve back to his lane, causing a head-on collision.

2. If you apply the foot brakes while driving and they do not work, try pumping them. If there is a small amount of braking power left, you may get enough response to stop the car (be certain you have not depressed the clutch pedal by mistake!). If the brakes are completely gone, shift into a lower gear so the engine will act as a brake, and apply the emergency brake, though it is effective only on the rear wheels. It will stop the car, but in a greater distance. Steer over to the right-hand side and drive on the shoulder, stopping as soon as you can.

Be careful about turning the ignition key off in order to stop the engine; on cars with the ignition switch on the steering column, you will lock the steering column if you turn the key all the way to the left. Cars with power steering will be *much harder* to steer with the engine off, but if you brace yourself and get a firm grip on the wheel, you should be able to steer the car.

3. If a car approaches you at night with its headlights on high beam, flick your lights to high beam and back to low beam; this reminder usually prompts the other driver to switch to low beam. If this does not work, avoid looking directly at his lights, which will blind you temporarily, and concentrate on looking at the right edge of the road. Slow down and steer as far to the right as possible. As soon as the car passes, put your lights on high beam as a safety measure so you can see what is ahead. Never try to "get even" with the other driver by putting your lights on high beam; you may blind him and cause a collision.

4. If the accelerator pedal sticks when you lift your foot off the gas, put the car into neutral gear and tap the pedal a few times to see if you can unstick it. If you need to stop immediately, turn the ignition key *slightly* to the left to turn off the engine (remember that turning the key completely to the left locks the steering wheel), and apply the brakes. Get a good grip on the steering wheel; if you have power steering, it will be much harder to turn. Push harder on the brake pedal; with the engine off, power brakes require much more force to stop the car. If the accelerator still sticks and the road ahead is clear, put your foot under it and try to lift it upwards, or ask your front-seat passenger to reach down to lift it. It is too dangerous for the driver to try to reach down to lift the accelerator.

5. If your car catches on fire, stop, get your fire extinguisher from the trunk, open the hood (most fires are near or in the engine), and

put out the fire. A portable extinguisher is useful when a fire first begins but is not effective for a car completely in flames. Stay far away from a flaming car because the gas tank may explode.

If you do not have a fire extinguisher, your action will depend on the cause of the fire. Use your jack handle to rip the wires apart if the trouble is shorted wires; a new wiring system is much cheaper than a new engine or a new car. Throw sand or soil on the engine; do likewise if the fire is caused by leaking gasoline. Do not put water on a gasoline fire, as it will only spread the fire.

6. Your car skids on wet pavement, plunges into a lake or river, and starts to sink. What can you do? Your first impulse is to open the door to get out. Water pressure on the outside of the door will probably make that escape impossible. Try rolling down a window and climbing out; open power windows immediately before they short out. Research shows a closed car will usually float for several minutes. If you do not panic, you can save your life; several minutes is a lot of time in an emergency. A car with the engine up front will sink nose first, so climb into the back seat. As the car fills with water, some air may be pushed to the rear near the roof. When the car is almost completely filled with water, a door may be opened, as the water pressure inside and outside is equalized.

7. You have a blowout on the superhighway. How will you handle this? If possible, use the right turn signals and get into the right-hand lane. If you are in the left lane when the tire blows out and there is a shoulder on the left side of the highway, you will be better off using your left turn signal and steering on to the shoulder on the left side of the highway. A blowout throws the car out of balance, which makes steering difficult. Reduce speed until you can safely drive onto the shoulder and stop. *Do not panic* and jam on the brakes; doing so may cause skidding and overturning. Turn on the four-way emergency flasher and use the red flasher on your spotlight to help prevent motorists from colliding into the rear of your car. Turn on the interior lights of the car at night and in inclement weather. If you need help, raise your hood. See Chapter 17, Tips on Easy Tasks, to put on the spare tire.

8. Your horn begins blowing and continues that awful noise for no apparent reason. What can you do? Open the trunk and get a pair of pliers, a wire cutter, or the jack handle. Open the hood, locate the horn, and use one of these tools to remove or cut the wires from the horn. This will stop the noise, and you can get the wires repaired later.

The problem was probably caused by shorted wires between the horn and the steering wheel.

9. If you are driving in a thunderstorm and lightning seems to be striking near you, stay in your car. A metal car with rubber tires is one of the safest places you can be during a thunderstorm. If the downpour gets so heavy you cannot see at least several car lengths in front of you, it is best to pull off the road onto the shoulder and wait until the storm passes. Turn off your headlights when you are on the shoulder of the road; another driver may be following your tail light and hit the rear of your car. Turn on your four-way emergency flasher; it may help to alert other drivers that you are stopped.

10. If you do not have a spare key, and your keys are in a locked car with the windows rolled up, then what can you do?

You might call a locksmith for help if you are in a city. Some service stations keep a wire or a flat metal tool for opening locked doors in such situations. But with the help of a wire coat hanger, you may be able to get into the car yourself. Straighten it out, and fashion a small hook on one end. Sometimes it is possible to work the front window down far enough to insert the wire and use the hook end to pull up the door lock button or the door handle. Another possibility is to insert the coat hanger wire below or through the rubber seal of the wing window (if you have one) to reach and raise the lock button; you may have to cut away the rubber insulation from a window to get in. If it becomes necessary to break a window, a wing window is less expensive to replace.

16

Ripoffs

REPAIRS

Unnecessary or exorbitant car repairs head the list of consumer gripes. Many car owners feel they are being ripped off, and frequently they are. On the other hand, the trouble could be a misunderstanding or no understanding before the repair work was undertaken.

If you are a newcomer to a community or are traveling away from home, you would be well advised to patronize a dealer who sells the same car or who represents the manufacturer of your car. A franchised dealer of a car manufacturer is less likely to make unnecessary repairs, and is more likely to have the part or parts you need. If you are dissatisfied, you will have some recourse through the manufacturer. An independent mechanic may take advantage of an out-of-town traveler, and you will have very little recourse.

Ask for and receive a written estimate for repairing the car; it is a protection both for the car owner and the repair shop. Sometimes there is a charge for the labor of making a diagnosis and arriving at an estimate, but this charge must be reasonable and should be disclosed on the estimate. Some states have consumer protection laws, which guarantee the motorist the right to a written estimate before the work is agreed upon if the repair is expected to exceed a certain amount. It is always less risky to get at least two bids for repair work when you are in a strange city. The repair shop should give you a bill itemizing the cost of the labor and all the parts—whether new or used—after the work is done. Remember that an estimate is just that; no mechanic can always know exactly what will be found upon opening up the engine or the transmission. Repair costs for the rest of the car are easier to estimate.

When you first discuss the repairs, tell the repair shop that you will want to see all the old parts taken off your car. Reputable shops are usually glad to give you old parts, such as valves, rings, plugs, points, and condenser. Other used parts, such as starters and alternators, have to be traded in to get a rebuilt unit. Some parts under warranty may have to be returned to the manufacturer or distributor, but you can ask to see all parts removed from your car. If you see the old parts taken off your car, then the mechanic has probably installed new parts. Some dishonest shops have been known to state that they put on a new part and to charge you for it, while in reality they did not replace the old part at all.

Older cars, less popular cars, and foreign cars sometimes need parts that are simply not available locally and may take some time to obtain from a distant source. You might start revising your plans to include possible delays when the mechanic expresses doubt about the availability of certain needed parts. Consider a rental car to save your vacation—you can pick up your repaired car at a later date.

Some larger cities and most states have a regulatory agency you can contact if you feel you have been cheated on a car repair. Locally you can contact the Better Business Bureau or the consumer relations division of the chamber of commerce. You can write the state attorney general's office, which will help you contact the appropriate state agency.

If auto parts are ordered through the mail but do not arrive or are not as represented, contact your local postmaster for information on filing a claim; also, you can complain to the Federal Trade Commission, Washington, D.C. 20580.

OIL

To avoid some common ripoffs, stay with your car when you stop at an unfamiliar service station, getting out and watching while the attendant services your car. Wait until the service operation is complete before you go to the rest room or go inside for a soft drink. The few extra minutes this takes are well worthwhile.

Through ignorance or intent, an attendant may open the hood and check the oil as soon as a car pulls into the station. He holds the dipstick in front of the unsuspecting motorist and with great authority announces that a quart of oil is needed. If the driver protests that the car should not need any oil, the dipstick right in front of his eyes provides the evidence that the oil level is low. As I mentioned before, since the engine has just stopped running and some oil still is circulating in the top of the engine, it is necessary to wait five or ten minutes for the oil to drain down into the crankcase. Then the oil level can be measured accurately and should show sufficient oil.

Let me say a word in defense of the station owner at this point. Most owners are honest and are trying to build a business, which cannot be done by dishonest practices. Some attendants do not realize that the oil needs time to drain down into the crankcase. When a quart of oil is added to an engine that already has enough, the engine simply throws out the excess oil. The only damage done is to your pocketbook. A variation of the "oil trick" is that the attendant does not push the dipstick down as far as it will go when he checks the oil.

You can easily avoid the oil ripoff by carrying out the four regular checks discussed in an earlier chapter, which include checking the oil yourself. When I stop for gas, I tell the attendant the kind of fuel I want and immediately inform him that the hood is okay. An honest attendant likes to hear this, as it saves him time and effort.

SHOCK ABSORBERS

Another ripoff to watch for is the "you need shock absorbers" ploy. You are more susceptible to this scheme on a toll highway or limited access highway where no other station is nearby. While your car is being serviced, you refresh yourself with a soft drink or visit the rest room. When you return, the attendant inquires how much farther you have to go. Whatever your reply, he will assert that your shocks are worn out, you will never make your destination, and you should not even drive a mile. The attendant just happens to have a lift available, and he can put on new shocks in a short time. You have heard that shocks do wear out and you have to make a decision about getting new ones installed, so what do you do?

Since it is true that any car part will wear out sooner or later, your shocks may be weak and need replacing, so that part of what the attendant says can be true. But he is telling a lie if he says you cannot drive another mile with worn shocks. A car has four shocks, one at each wheel; they do get weaker and less effective with age and use, but they do not normally break or wear out all at once. In fact, you could drive the car with all four shocks removed, but not very fast because the car would sway excessively and be unstable.

If this situation happens to you, thank the attendant for informing you that your shocks are getting weak and then proceed down the road, driving slower and more cautiously. At the first opportunity, or when you arrive home, get an opinion from another mechanic to see if you really need new shocks. If you do, check the local newspaper—shocks are frequently advertised on sale.

A variation of the shock scheme is for the attendant to take an oil can and squirt oil on one of the shocks, so that it leaks on the pavement from the outside of the shock. The attendant feigns alarm when you return: your shock is leaking oil, and you absolutely cannot drive another mile until he replaces all your shocks! The truth is that a shock absorber does contain a small amount of oil to make an airtight seal between the plunger and the walls of the cylinder, but it is not full of oil. Remember that shock absorbers do wear out eventually and will need replacing, but they do not wear out all at once (see Chapter 8, Brakes, Steering, and Shocks).

ADDITIVES

Millions of car owners in this country have problems sooner or later; inventors and engineers are constantly seeking improvements in solving car problems. Unfortunately, gyp artists are also inventing "improvements" that merely fleece the public. Some additive products are helpful, some do no good, and some are even harmful to your car.

Supplementary additives for the engine oil may not hurt the engine, and they can be genuinely useful in certain cases. Remember a top grade (SE) engine oil already has beneficial additives.

In addition to additives for oil, dozens of additives are available to give a certain benefit or improvement to almost every part of the car: some are added to the gas, some to the engine through the carburetor, some are placed in the radiator, and there are even some for the battery. I do not endorse or condemn the many products available; a few that have proved beneficial beyond any doubt are mentioned in this book. Products that claim secret ingredients that will do miracle jobs should be questioned. Before you spend money on additives to cure your car's problem, check an unbiased authority, such as *Consumer Reports*. Another source of helpful advice is your honest, reputable mechanic.

17

Tips on Easy Tasks

I have already explained how to check the liquid level in the battery, the oil level in the engine, the liquid level in the radiator, and the air pressure in the tires in the chapter on Four Regular Checks. Here are some other easy tasks you can do with a minimum of tools, mechanical ability, and expertise:

1. Servicing the air cleaner
2. Removing battery corrosion
3. Using jumper cables
4. Checking the brake fluid level
5. Putting on the spare tire
6. Checking the power steering fluid level
7. Checking the automatic transmission fluid
8. Filling the windshield washer reservoir
9. Replacing windshield wiper blades
10. Replacing fuses
11. Replacing the turn signal flasher
12. Replacing the four-way hazard flasher
13. Replacing light bulbs

SERVICING THE AIR CLEANER

On most cars the air cleaner is inside a round can, usually located above the carburetor. The round lid is usually held on with a wing nut(s) that must be removed. Lift the lid off and remove the round paper filter element to examine it. Replace the element when it is dark on the outside and the inside.

Refer to your Owner's Manual to learn approximately how many miles you can drive before the element needs changing. Your manual gives a good rule of thumb, but remember that the more dirt roads you drive on, the sooner the element will get dirty. A car driven only on pavement can go about 20,000 miles before it needs a new air cleaner element, but a car driven on dirt roads should be inspected about every 1,000 miles. The first time you service the air cleaner yourself, ask your regular mechanic's opinion if you have any doubts about whether the filter element is dirty enough to need changing.

Buy a new air cleaner element from an auto parts store by specifying the year and make of your car, or take the old element with you. Before installing it, clean the container with a rag dipped in kerosene or lightweight oil, such as 3-in-One oil or sewing machine oil. Either side can be installed face up unless the element indicates a top side, so you cannot put it in wrong. Replace the lid and tighten the wing nut securely to avoid a rattle. Some cars, such as the Chevrolet Vega, have an air cleaner unit that cannot be taken apart, and you have to purchase the entire metal can unit containing the filter. Several nuts must be removed to make this change. Use a small, adjustable crescent wrench or a socket wrench to perform this task.

REMOVING BATTERY CORROSION

Each battery has two terminals, a positive and a negative. These terminals are located on the top of the battery or on the side near the top. The battery cables are attached to the terminals and carry the required voltage to the electrical system. Corrosion happens naturally, and is not an indication of a problem, but it can prevent the car from starting when you least expect it. So keep it off your battery terminals and metal battery clamps by removing it periodically.

Battery corrosion

Do not park your car on a paved driveway when you remove corrosion, as you may stain it. This is the procedure:

Make sure that all the vent caps are covering the cells (soda water getting into the cell may cause an explosion or a violent reaction and splash you with acid). Mix a concentrated solution of ordinary baking soda and faucet water (approximately five tablespoons of soda to one-half cup of water), and pour this solution on the corrosion, using an old toothbrush or wire brush to scrub away the corrosion. If the battery is in the engine compartment, you can use a water hose or a sprinkling can to rinse off all the corrosion and remaining soda, leaving the metal parts clean. Dry off the terminals with a paper towel or cloth. A film of petroleum jelly or wheel bearing grease applied to the outside of the terminals and the metal battery clamps will help prevent the accumulation of corrosion.

If your battery has been neglected for one or two years and the terminals are thoroughly covered with corrosion, it is best to remove the clamps with a wrench or pliers and clean them and the battery terminals with baking soda. Then use sandpaper or a special battery terminal cleaning tool to scour the metal inside the clamps and around the terminals. Replace the clamps, tighten, and apply grease.

QUESTION: Can Coca-Cola be used instead of baking soda to remove corrosion from batteries? No, Coca-Cola is not strong enough.

USING JUMPER CABLES

Jumper cables are colored red and black to help you place them correctly. Use a helper battery of the same voltage as the dead battery. For example, if the dead battery is twelve volts (one with six vent caps), the helper car must have a twelve-volt battery. You will normally have another person to help you when you are using a helper battery from another vehicle.

Identify the positive and negative terminals on the dead battery and on the helper battery. The positive terminals will be labeled with the letters POS or P, or a plus sign ($+$), and the negative terminals can be identified by the letters NEG or N, or a minus sign ($-$).

Caution! Do not attempt to use the jumper cables if you cannot identify the positive and negative terminals of both batteries. Get a professional mechanic to help you.

Follow this procedure when jump-starting. For simplicity, I will refer to the *helper car* as A and the *dead battery car* as B:

a. Position the two vehicles so they are *not* touching.

b. Remove the vent caps from both batteries and cover the vents with cloth.

c. Turn off the engine in helper car A, so no damage can occur to its electrical system if the cables are not connected properly. (If car A does not have enough power to start car B, get another helper battery—or crank car A using its own battery and take your chances on an improper connection.)

d. In car B, set the parking brake and place automatic transmission in "park" (or put manual transmission in "neutral").

e. Attach a black end of one jumper cable to the negative terminal of the dead battery in car B, and the other black end to the negative terminal of the battery in car A.

f. Attach a red end of the remaining cable to the positive terminal of the dead battery in car B (have the ignition key inserted and be ready to start car B before the last connection is made).

g. Attach the other red end of the cable to the positive terminal of the battery in car A. Turn the ignition key in car B. As soon as the engine starts, remove the jumper cables in reverse sequence, making certain not to touch the cables to each other.

h. After jump-starting, be certain to replace the vent caps.

Caution! I cannot overemphasize the importance of following safety precautions when using jumper cables. Do not smoke—any spark or open flame is dangerous, as the battery generates explosive hydrogen gas. Wear eye protection. Avoid letting battery fluid contact skin, eyes, fabrics, or painted surfaces. Never jump-start a car with a frozen battery, as the battery may explode. Look into the vent openings to check the liquid level if you suspect a frozen battery, and do not attempt to start the car with jumper cables if you see ice or cannot see liquid.

CHECKING THE BRAKE FLUID LEVEL

The hydraulic brake fluid reserve container is located in the engine compartment directly in front of the driver. The container is elongated

Brake fluid reservoir

and is mounted on the fire wall. A wire clip usually holds the lid on, but some lids have screw caps. Take a screwdriver and pry the wire fastener to one side to free the lid, then remove it. The container holding the brake fluid is divided in the center. Each of the two compartments should be full to the top of the rim.

Add brake fluid as needed if the liquid level is low. Ask for the very best quality when buying brake fluid—your life may depend on your brakes, so do not scrimp on this item. Replace the lid and the clip, and that is all there is to it. Some foreign cars have two small containers with a lid on each mounted in front of the fire wall on the driver's side. Both should be filled.

Brake fluid has a peculiar odor. Learn to recognize this odor, and have your brakes checked immediately if you smell it.

PUTTING ON THE SPARE TIRE

Make sure the car is parked on level ground, and put chock blocks in front and back of any one tire other than the one that is flat. The car could roll forward or backward when the bumper jack is lifting it.

Wheel chocks

Put the emergency brake on, and place the gear shift in "park," or with manual transmission in first gear. Remove the spare, the jack, and the jack handle from the trunk. Look on the inside of the trunk lid or in the Owner's Manual for instructions on using the bumper jack. Many cars have a slot or groove for the jack to fit in, either under the front or back bumper or on the side of the car below the door panels. This makes the jack less likely to slip.

Use the jack handle to pry off the hub cap or wheel disc, revealing the lug bolts and/or lug nuts. While some cars have lug bolts that screw into the wheel hub and hold the wheel on, most cars have lug bolts that are permanently attached to the wheel hub. Lug nuts screw on these permanent bolts, holding the wheel on. Lug nuts have a right-hand thread on practically all cars. Before jacking up the car, use the jack handle or a large X wrench to "crack" (barely loosen) the nut on each lug bolt. To loosen, turn the lug nuts in a counterclockwise direction.

Some Chrysler cars have left-hand threads on the lug nuts of the rear wheels, as may some older cars of other makes. This is rare, but you may encounter it. A left-hand thread is indicated by an "L" stamped into the end of the lug bolt. Examine the end of the lug bolt carefully for an "L" before trying to turn the nut counterclockwise. Such left-hand-threaded lug nuts must be turned clockwise to loosen them.

Place the small lever on the jack frame in the UP position. Operate the jack until the wheel is raised an inch or so off the ground, and remove the lug nuts. Drop the nuts into the hub cap or wheel disc to avoid getting them dirty or losing them. Take off the wheel and install the spare, putting the lug nuts back on with the beveled edge *toward* the car, the same way the nuts faced when you took them off.

Using bumper jack

Using X wrench

Tighten the lug nuts snugly, but do not use your full strength. Move the small lever on the jack frame to DOWN and lower the jack. When the wheel touches ground solidly, go back to the lug nuts and use your full strength to tighten them. Do not tighten the lug nuts going consecutively around the wheel hub. It is better to tighten a lug nut, then tighten the one opposite it, and so on until all are tight. Replace the hub cap or wheel disc and remove the jack. Then, obviously, have the flat tire repaired.

CHECKING THE POWER STEERING FLUID LEVEL

The level of fluid in the power steering unit should be checked every time the car is serviced, but you can double check it yourself quite easily. It should be done in the morning before the car is driven that day.

Open the hood and locate the power steering pump, which is mounted on the engine and is driven with a pulley and a belt. The pump is easily identified by the two hoses leading from it to the steering gear assembly at the lower end of the steering column. A lid with a measuring stick is attached to the top of the pump. Remove the lid. The measuring stick has a cold-full mark and a hot-full mark or similar markings. The fluid should be up to the cold-full mark.

If the fluid is low, use a funnel and pour in the proper fluid until the full mark is reached. Do not overfill! Refer to your Owner's Manual for the proper fluid for power steering. My manual recommends a power steering fluid sold by the car manufacturer. My manual also says to substitute automatic transmission fluid if power steering

Power steering fluid dipstick and container

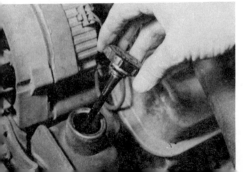

fluid is not available. Follow the information given in your Owner's Manual. Replace the lid.

CHECKING THE AUTOMATIC TRANSMISSION FLUID LEVEL

The fluid level in the automatic transmission should be checked every time the car is serviced, but you can check the fluid level easily. Drive the car five or ten miles to bring the transmission fluid up to normal operating temperature; then open the hood and let the engine idle. Locate the transmission fluid dipstick back near the fire wall; it resembles the engine oil dipstick. Pull the dipstick out, wipe it off, and replace. Then pull the dipstick out again and read the level indicated. You will need a long, flexible hose and funnel in order to pour fluid into the transmission. Refer to your Owner's Manual for the right kind of fluid. If the dipstick shows the fluid is low, a pint or less should bring the level to the full mark. Automatic transmission fluid is sold only in quart cans, so you will have some left over for the next time. Do not overfill! Remember that to get an accurate reading the engine must be warm and idling, and the car must be on a level surface.

Some car owners check the transmission fluid level themselves, but take the car to a service station to have transmission fluid added, since this requires the purchase of a special funnel and hose. This makes sense, as you should not have to add fluid more than once or twice a year.

FILLING THE WINDSHIELD WASHER RESERVOIR

Under the hood, you will find a plastic container with a small rubber hose leading to the windshield wiper motor that is mounted on the fire wall. (Do not confuse this plastic container with the one on a closed cooling system, which has a rubber hose leading to the top of the radiator.) Normally, once a month is a good time to glance at the reservoir to see that you have plenty of liquid in it.

You can see the level of the liquid in the container through the translucent plastic. Simply remove the plastic lid to add liquid to the container. Water alone will do a fair job of cleaning your windshield in summer, but a special cleaning solution is much better. In the winter, you must add a special antifreeze solution.

REPLACING WINDSHIELD WIPER BLADES

Most American cars have windshield wiper blades with the words "Anco" or "Trico" on them. You may be able to get an Anco or Trico blade to fit your foreign car if the blades need replacing; an auto parts store has a complete list of which blades will fit which cars. Otherwise you will have to get a replacement from the parts department of your car dealer.

With Anco or Trico blades, a rubber refill element is inexpensive and easy to install. When you buy the refill element, you will need to know the brand name, the length of the wiper blade, and the make and year of your car—or just bring the old blade to the store.

Follow the instructions on the box containing the refill element. An Anco blade usually has two small red buttons on the blade holder. Push these down to pull the old rubber element out and put the new one in. On a Trico blade, lift the blade up and pull the old rubber element out. You may need a pair of pliers for this task. Then slide the new element into place.

Some cars have hidden wipers that disappear between the hood and the windshield. Turn on the ignition key and the wiper switch to operate the electric motor and bring the wipers out of the hidden compartment. Stop the wipers by turning off the ignition key while the blades are in plain view on the windshield. Now you can get to the blade to identify the brand name and to change the rubber element. On hidden wiper blades there is a removable pin in the center: remove this pin to take the entire blade unit off the wiper arm. The job of replacing the rubber element will be much easier with the blade in your hands. Next put the blade back on the same way it came off and replace the pin.

Worn out wiper blade and refills

Let me stress that if your car has Anco or Trico blades you do not need to buy complete blades; get only the rubber refill element. You will probably have to buy an entire unit if your car does not have Anco or Trico blades. Specify the make and model of your car and the wiper blade length. Sears sells a complete blade unit and refills. The complete wiper unit will be more expensive than simply getting a rubber refill element, but when the rubber element wears out, you will only need to get a low-cost refill.

REPLACING FUSES

Read your Owner's Manual to locate the fuse block containing the fuses for the electrical system. On some cars, the fuse block is located against the fire wall under the dash.

You will find several fuses of different sizes for particular purposes. My car has nine fuses rated 10A (amperes), 20A, and 25A. The various circuits controlled by the fuses will be indicated in the manual and may be labeled on the fuse block, for example: Heater, A/C, Wiper, Radio, Back-up, Tail, and Ltr (lighter). Each fuse may be linked to more than one component. Your Owner's Manual contains further information on fuses and circuits.

What causes fuses to blow? Sometimes the cause is unknown. Perhaps a loose connection caused the wires to heat up or a surge of electricity blew the fuse. An acquaintance of mine in a northern state turned on his windshield wipers after a sleet storm. The wipers were held by the ice on the windshield, and the fuse blew to protect the wiper motor, which would have been damaged.

If you can find the trouble that caused a fuse to blow, try to correct it before putting in a new fuse. Take a small (about 3-inch) screwdriver and carefully pry the blown fuse out of the fuse block. The

Fuse block

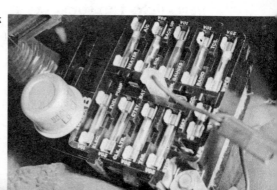

blown fuse usually will be blackened and the metal strip on the side, or inside of it, will be split. Many auto fuses have a glass body, so be careful not to break it when you are prying it out. After you remove the blown fuse, install a new one of the same size. Use your fingers to press gently on the new fuse until it pops into the fuse holder on the fuse block. If the fuse immediately blows again, there is a short circuit somewhere that will have to be repaired by a mechanic.

I recommend that you keep in the glove compartment spare fuses of all the sizes used in your car. Having a spare fuse when needed can save you much time and inconvenience. Any malfunction in the electrical system, such as inoperative lights, horn, or windshield wipers, may simply be the result of a blown fuse. Always check the fuses before taking any further action, since you may be able to solve the problem by yourself in a minute.

Caution! Do not substitute a bolt or wrap aluminum foil around an old, blown fuse. Doing so could cause damage to the wiring.

REPLACING THE TURN SIGNAL FLASHER

If only the left-hand or the right-hand signal works, the cause is probably just a burned-out bulb, which is easy to replace (check the fuse first!). If both bulbs are out at the same time, then the turn signal flasher probably needs replacing.

Look under the dash for a round (slightly larger in diameter than a quarter) or rectangular (about $1\frac{1}{4} \times \frac{3}{4} \times 1\frac{1}{3}$ inches) metal can plugged into sockets on wires or on the fuse block. The Owner's Manual may show the location of the flasher, which has two metal male connectors. Pull the flasher straight out to disconnect it. Buy a new flasher from an auto parts store and plug it in.

REPLACING THE FOUR-WAY HAZARD FLASHER

The four-way hazard flasher looks like the turn signal flasher, and it is easy to get the two of them confused. My car has the four-way hazard flasher located on the fuse block, but the turn signal flasher plugs into sockets on wires under the dash. Refer to your Owner's Manual for the location of the four-way hazard flasher. Pull straight out to unplug the old flasher. Purchase a new flasher at your auto parts supply store and plug it in.

REPLACING LIGHT BULBS

Refer to your Owner's Manual for the bulb number or type you will need to replace a burned-out bulb; or remove the burned-out bulb and take it to the auto parts store to get the proper replacement. According to make and year there is wide variation in cars as to the location and fixture type of lights in the passenger compartment, glove compartment, trunk, hood, and other places. Therefore, specific instructions on changing bulbs for these locations cannot be given. Usually you will not have any difficulty changing them. On most cars a dash light can be replaced by reaching underneath and behind the dash to remove the old bulb and put in a new one.

Headlights and taillights are a little more complicated to change. Practically all cars have sealed-beam headlights. To remove the sealed-beam unit, a piece of decorative chrome or other material surrounding the headlight first must be removed, using a medium-size Phillips screwdriver. After the chrome is removed, you can see other screws holding a metal ring that fits snugly around the sealed-beam unit. Remove these screws also.

Removing headlight

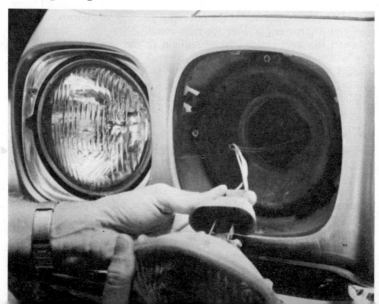

Caution! Do not turn the two screws that you can see before any chrome is removed. They probably have a spring under them. These two screws are located at the top and at the side of the headlight, and they are used to aim the headlight. The top screw adjusts the headlight in an up-and-down motion and the side screw adjusts the headlight in a side-to-side motion. You can easily identify the two spring adjustment screws; they are visible when the decorative chrome is in place. A mechanic can adjust your headlights without removing the decorative chrome.

If you make the mistake of turning these aiming screws, you will have to take your car to a garage that has the proper equipment for aiming the headlights after you replace the burned-out sealed-beam unit, since aiming the headlights correctly is not a job for the do-it-yourselfer. Some states require periodic vehicle inspections, during which the headlights are checked for proper aim. This is an important safety consideration, and you will want your headlights to be aimed correctly whether your state has vehicle inspections or not.

The sealed-beam unit will be free after you remove the decorative chrome and the metal band. Carefully move the unit forward until you can remove the electric plug and cord from the back of the headlight.

Purchase a new sealed-beam unit with the same number as the old one. The number cast into the glass of the unit will be 1 or 2. If your car has four headlights, the outside two lamps will be No. 2 and the inside lamps will be No. 1. Make sure the replacement sealed-beam unit is the same diameter as the old unit by taking the burned-out unit with you when you purchase the new unit.

Install the new sealed-beam headlight in the reverse order of the way you removed the old unit. Be careful to get the screws started straight and not cross-threaded. A little soap on the screws will usually make them go in easily. I keep a small bar of soap (the kind supplied by motels) in my toolbox for this purpose. If you hold the bar of soap firmly and rake the screw across it, the threads will pick up enough soap to lubricate the screw.

To replace a taillight, the procedure varies with different cars. On some cars, you will need a Phillips screwdriver to remove a translucent plastic piece that may be red or amber in color. Then you can reach the individual bulb that is defective. Some bulbs have two filaments (rear brake and normal lighting, and front turn signal and normal lighting). Even though only one filament is burned out, the bulb should be replaced. Remove the old bulb by turning counterclockwise about one-eighth turn. You may have to push in on the bulb slightly to turn it. Be certain to install an exact replacement of any burned-out bulb.

On other cars, you will find a plastic fixture that contains the tail-light inside the trunk. Turn the end of the fixture counterclockwise about one-eighth turn to free it. You can reach the bulb when the fixture comes out. Remove and replace the bulb as explained above.

For the other rear bulbs, such as the back-up and license plate lights, make a visual examination to determine what you have to do to reach the bulb so you can remove and replace it.

In taking apart any mechanism, note carefully where each screw belongs and the sequence in which components fit together.

18

Tips on Medium Tasks

You have to have the proper tools before you attempt most of these medium tasks, though you can occasionally substitute an all-purpose tool, *e.g.,* a small adjustable wrench, for a specific tool. I recommend that you buy a set of metric auto wrenches if you have a foreign car or an American car that requires metric tools. Sometimes auto parts stores have these on sale and that is a good time to buy and save money; the cost varies depending on the number and quality of the tools. If your car is American, especially an older model, you may need certain wrenches and tools labeled in inches or fractions to work on it. Buy only those you must have, because within a few years all new American cars will require metric tools.

Here are some medium tasks you should be able to perform if you have the right tools and equipment, some mechanical ability, and the time and patience to do them. They really are not difficult, and the novice who thinks he or she is all thumbs should not avoid trying them.

1. Repacking the front wheel bearings—drum brakes
2. Repacking the front wheel bearings—disc brakes
3. Flushing the cooling system
4. Replacing the thermostat
5. Changing the hoses
6. Lubricating the car
7. Changing the oil and the oil filter
8. Changing drive belts

REPACKING THE FRONT WHEEL BEARINGS—
DRUM BRAKES

Things you will need:

a. A one-pound can of Wolf's Head Lube super-duty and wheel bearing grease or the equivalent, or whatever your Owner's Manual recommends. Be certain the grease is water resistant; an inferior grease will melt under the ordinary operating temperatures of the hub and get on the brakes, causing serious trouble.

b. Two 2-inch-long cotter pins, ⅛-inch in diameter

c. Two new grease seals

d. Small can of kerosene (to soak bearings, nut, and washers)

e. Ballpeen hammer with wooden handle

f. Adjustable pliers (slip-joint type)

g. Large slot-blade screwdriver

h. Jack stand

i. Lots of old rags

Removing dust cap on drum brake hub

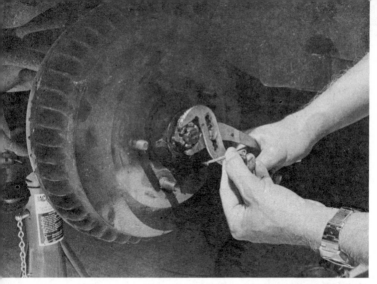

Removing nut (removed cotter pin in left hand)

Removing outer bearing

Removing wheel hub

Removing drum brake grease seal

Washing bearing in kerosene (grease seal at lower left)

Greasing bearing

Normally, the bearings need repacking every twelve months or 10,000 miles; double check with your Owner's Manual. Set the emergency brake and place chock blocks in front and back of one rear wheel. Use the bumper jack to lift a front wheel off the ground. Use a jack stand under the front suspension (a jack stand is used to hold up securely either the front or the rear of a car that has been lifted with a bumper jack). Never use concrete blocks or just a bumper jack to hold up the car while you work on it—concrete blocks are brittle and may collapse suddenly, and a bumper jack can fail without warning.

Remove the wheel. Spin the hub to detect noise, which indicates faulty bearings. Use the hammer, screwdriver, and pliers to remove the metal dust cap covering the hub; then use the pliers to remove the cotter pin. Unscrew the nut counterclockwise, and put the nut and washer in the kerosene can.

Pull slightly on the round wheel hub. As the hub comes towards you, the outer bearing will fall in your hand. Put the bearing in the kerosene. Remove the hub completely and place it on a flat surface with the inside facing down. Use the wooden handle of the ballpeen hammer to knock out the grease seal, allowing the inner bearing to come out.

Caution! Do not drive the grease seal out with a metal object because bearing damage will result.

Use kerosene to clean all the old grease off both bearings and out of the hub. Wipe off the kerosene, and then blow the bearings dry with a vacuum cleaner. Inspect all bearings for pits and surface scars. Any bearing damage means new bearings are needed. In that case, I suggest that you grease the damaged bearing and reassemble the hub and wheel, and then go to a reputable mechanic and get him to inspect all front wheel bearings and replace needed parts. Damaged bearings mean the bearing race or track that they move in may be damaged, and replacing this is a job for the professional.

If you find no bearing damage, take the inner bearing first and thoroughly work the wheel bearing grease into all parts of the bearing and the hub. Be generous; grease is inexpensive.

Replace the inner bearing and use the head of the hammer to put in a new grease seal. Put the wheel hub back on the axle. Coat the outer bearing with grease and replace the bearing in the wheel hub. Replace the washer and nut, tightening the nut as far as possible, and then turning it backwards just enough to align the holes for the cotter pin. Put in a new cotter pin and spread the ends so that they appear the way you found the old cotter pin. Use the hammer to replace the dust cap on the hub. The wheel hub should rotate easily. Put the wheel back on, remove the jack stand and the jack, and repeat the operation on the other front wheel.

   Caution! The cotter pin prevents the nut from unscrewing and the wheel from coming off. Failure to follow instructions can be hazardous to the operator and others. Be careful not to get any grease on the brake linings. After repacking your wheels, ask a reputable mechanic to check them if you have any doubts about whether the job has been done properly.

REPACKING THE FRONT WHEEL BEARINGS—DISC BRAKES

Things you will need:

   a. All the items listed above for drum brake wheels
   b. Two 1 x 4 x 12-inch boards
   c. Four retaining pin nuts
   d. Piece of flexible wire 18 inches long for hanging the caliper
   e. Nut driver or socket wrench

Wheel hub and disc brake

Removing retainer pin (top pin still has nut on)

Hanging the caliper from front suspension

Using ballpeen hammer to knock out grease seal

Removing inner bearing

Replacing wheel hub

Replacing outer bearing

Replacing cotter pin

Read the previous section on repacking the front wheel bearings—drum brakes. Follow the same procedure to jack up the car and remove the wheel, the dust cap, the cotter pin, and the nut and washer. Use a screwdriver to pry both mounting-pin retaining nuts off. (These nuts are usually held on with friction, and the mounting pins are not threaded.) Remove the two mounting pins that hold the caliper by using a pair of pliers—giving a twisting, turning, pulling motion. Lift the caliper off the disc. Use the wire to hang the caliper from the front suspension. Never let the caliper hang by the brake line.

Pull the disc wheel hub outward and the outer wheel bearing will fall into your hands. Put the bearing in the kerosene can. Place the wheel hub on the wooden boards inside down with the boards near the outer edge of the disc, leaving the center of the hub unobstructed. Use the wooden handle of the ballpeen hammer to knock the grease seal out; then the inner bearing will come out. Invert the whole hub to remove the inner bearing.

Follow the same process as with drum brake wheels to clean the old grease off, inspect the bearings, apply bearing grease, and replace the inner bearing and new grease seal. Next put the wheel hub back on the axle, coat the outer wheel bearing with grease and replace it along with the washer, nut, and cotter pin as explained above.

Replace the caliper and the two caliper mounting pins. Put the two new retaining pin nuts on the ends of the retaining pins by applying pressure with a nut driver or a socket from a socket set.

Replace the dust seal at the hub. Replace the wheel, remove the jack stand and jack, and proceed to the other front wheel. Follow the preceding cautionary note.

FLUSHING THE COOLING SYSTEM

Things you will need:

a. Needle-nose pliers
b. Water hose
c. Antifreeze solution (see your Owner's Manual for the amount of coolant needed)
d. Distilled water

Park the car on a city street or somewhere other than your paved driveway. Otherwise the rusty water from the radiator may cause red iron stains, or the old antifreeze may kill your grass. If yours is a conventional cooling system, remove the radiator cap, start the car, and let the engine idle for about ten minutes to bring it to operating temperature; then shut off the engine. Use the pliers to loosen the petcock at the bottom of the radiator by turning the winged screw counterclockwise. After you loosen the petcock, put the pliers down and use your fingers to turn the screw valve as far open as it will go, but do not force the screw valve; it is not supposed to come completely out, so stop just when it gets difficult to turn. Be careful of getting scalded! The water from the radiator will be hot. Keep the radiator cap off so the liquid will flow better; then crank the engine again and let it idle.

Have your water hose hooked up, ready to replenish the water in the cooling system as soon as all the liquid is drained out. This step is called flushing the system. Remember that the engine is idling, so keep your hands away from the spinning fan blades.

When you have filled the radiator full and it has drained out—do this twice—stop the engine. Close the petcock with your fingers and then use the pliers to tighten the winged screw nut so the petcock will not leak. Do not put all your strength on tightening the screw because you may strip the threads.

Take the proper amount of antifreeze or antifreeze-and-water solution and prepare to pour the solution into the radiator. Start the engine before you pour coolant into the radiator; you may damage the engine if you pour cold liquid into the radiator when the engine is hot and not running. Fill the radiator until the core is covered, and then stop the engine and replace the radiator cap.

The radiator cap on some sealed systems is labeled "Do Not Open." Flushing the system is an exception, so remove the cap and start the engine. Then follow the same steps as with a conventional cooling system. Finally, empty the plastic container of coolant and refill with new coolant.

You may use faucet water in flushing the cooling system because of the convenience; the water is passing through the engine and flushing out sediment and rust. But, as stated before, rainwater or distilled water mixed with antifreeze is best for your cooling system, and should be used for the final fill-up.

REPLACING THE THERMOSTAT

Things you will need:

    a. New thermostat of the proper size and temperature rating
    b. Socket set or box wrenches
    c. New gasket
    d. Gasket cement

The thermostat is located in the engine block where the top radiator hose connects to the engine. Drain and save the coolant. Use the socket set or box wrenches to remove the nuts holding the thermostat housing that is attached to the radiator hose. You may have to remove the alternator bracket or other metal parts.

Remove the old thermostat and gasket, and clean the recessed portion of the housing so the new thermostat will fit properly. Place the new thermostat in the block in the same direction as the old thermostat. Apply gasket cement to both sides of the new gasket. Install the gasket and replace the thermostat housing. Tighten the nuts after replacing all brackets. Don't forget to replace the coolant.

Caution! Install the thermostat with the proper side facing inward. A thermostat is usually marked to show the proper direction in which it should be installed.

CHANGING THE HOSES

Things you will need:

    a. New hose or hoses
    b. Two new clamps for each hose (screw type)
    c. Adjustable slip-joint pliers
    d. Screwdriver

I suggest that you change the two radiator hoses every two years. First drain and save the coolant from the radiator. Use the pliers to remove the clamps from the hose to be replaced. The original clamps are probably the spring-steel type designed for trench pliers, and you should be able to remove them with adjustable slip-joint pliers. Pull firmly on the hose, using a twisting, turning motion until both ends are free.

Install the new hose and tighten the new clamps with a screwdriver. Replace the coolant in the radiator.

LUBRICATING THE CAR

Things you will need:

    a. Grease gun (pistol type)
    b. Cartridge of grease to fit the gun
    c. Two jack stands or two metal car ramps, each with a capacity of 2,500 pounds, or at least half the weight of your car
    d. Tools as needed
    e. Rags
    f. Auto creeper (optional)

Auto creeper

An auto creeper is not essential, but it is handy for the amateur mechanic. It is a flat, boardlike device with four small wheels, and enables the operator to lie on his back and move easily to various locations under the car when greasing it or performing other service work.

Normally, a lube job and a change of oil and oil filter are performed at the same time. If you do these tasks yourself, it is the ideal time to check the various other fluids in the car: battery, radiator, transmission, brake, and power steering.

I suggest you go to a service station and have grease fittings installed if you have a new car that came from the factory with "plugs" instead of grease fittings; fittings are necessary to grease a car. If your car already has grease fittings, then proceed. Consult your Owner's Manual to learn how many grease fittings are on your car, as the number varies a great deal depending on the make and year of the car.

Jack stands (grease gun and oil filter wrench in center)

Car ramps

Set the emergency brake, put chock blocks in front and back of a rear wheel, and use the bumper jack to lift the front, one side at a time, for your jack stands. Or drive the car up on the car ramps, set the emergency brake, and chock a rear wheel.

Caution! Never work under a car held up by a bumper jack or concrete blocks! The bumper jack may give way with no warning, and concrete blocks are brittle and may collapse suddenly.

Use a rag to wipe off each grease fitting. Press the grease gun hose connector onto each fitting and hold the connector on with one hand, operating the trigger with the other hand to apply grease to the fitting. You should pump grease into the fitting until you see the boot begin to expand. Stop! It is not necessary to force grease to come out of the joint. Be certain to grease *all* fittings; do not neglect a single one.

Remove the jack stands from the front, or back the car off the ramp. Place the jack stands under the rear axle, or back the rear wheels up on the car ramps, chock a front wheel, and then check the differential, which is situated between the two rear wheels.

Grease gun in use

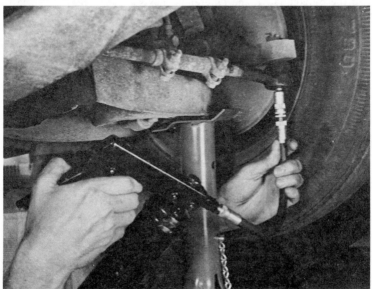

Differential with plug removed

Remove the filler plug on the differential; location of the plug varies —look for it. You may need a special tool or wrench. For example, a ⅜-inch drive handle for a socket set fits some General Motors cars, while other cars may require an open-end or box wrench. When the plug is removed, stick your little finger in the opening to check the level of the differential grease. The grease should be ½-inch below the top of the opening. Go to a service station to have differential grease added if the grease level is too low. The station has a pressure gun and the proper grease, and there is no easy way for the car owner to add grease to the differential. If the differential has sufficient grease, replace the plug and remove the jack stands or take the car off the ramps.

CHANGING THE OIL AND THE OIL FILTER

Things you will need:

    a. Oil filter wrench
    b. New oil filter (proper number for your car)
    c. Plastic dishpan or container that will hold up to two gallons (for the used oil)
    d. Two jack stands or two metal ramps, each with a capacity of 2,500 pounds, or at least half the weight of your car
    e. Box wrench to fit oil drain plug
    f. Oil (the required number of quarts of the proper oil)
    g. Pouring spout, or funnel and can opener
    h. Wheel bearing grease
    i. Rags
    j. Auto creeper (optional)

Some people consider changing the oil and changing the oil filter as two separate tasks, but I consider them as one task because I recommend that you always change the oil filter when you change the oil.

Set the emergency brake and put chock blocks in front and back of one rear wheel. Use the bumper jack to lift the front, one side at a time, so you can place your jack stands under the front. Or drive the front wheels on the car ramps, set the emergency brake, and chock a rear wheel. Let the engine idle for five minutes; then turn it off.

Caution! Never work under a car held up by a bumper jack! The bumper jack is not safe when you have to get under the car. Do not use concrete blocks to hold up the car, as they are brittle and may collapse suddenly.

Box wrench removing oil drain plug

Oil filter wrench secured to oil filter

Place the dishpan under the oil drain plug, and use your box wrench to remove the plug. After all the oil drains out, replace the oil drain plug and tighten. Then place the dishpan beneath the oil filter, and use your oil filter wrench to unscrew it and remove it. Apply wheel bearing grease on the rubber seal of the new oil filter. Install the new filter and tighten it with your hands. Do not use the oil filter wrench to tighten the oil filter or you will have great difficulty in removing the oil filter the next time.

Open the oil filler cap on top of the engine and use the oil can pouring spout to add the necessary quarts of oil, or use the can opener on the cans and add oil through the funnel. As some oil will usually be spilled with a pouring spout, I strongly urge you to use a funnel to pour oil into the engine if your car is a Chevrolet Vega. Any spilled oil goes into the alternator on the Vega (and perhaps on some other cars) and can cause expensive repair bills. Replace the oil cap filter.

Crank the engine and let it idle for five minutes while you look underneath the car to see if any oil is leaking at the drain plug or at the new filter. Bury the old oil, or put it in empty milk containers and place it in the garbage.

Caution! Some discount auto parts stores sell a device called an "electric-drill-powered oil changer." By attaching an electric drill to a special pump device and lowering a hose into the oil dipstick sheath, a person can pump the oil out of his engine to save the trouble of getting underneath the car. Do not buy this gadget! No pump can completely remove all the dirty oil from the crankcase, and the oil remaining will contaminate the clean oil that you add. When you remove the drain plug from a warm engine, the oil will flow out rapidly, taking with it any metal particles, sludge, and other materials that have settled in the bottom of the crankcase, but an oil pump will not remove all of this material.

Inspect the PCV (positive crankcase ventilation) valve at each oil change. The PCV valve helps to cut down on air pollution, and must be clean in order to maintain efficient engine operation. The location of PCV valves varies with different makes and models of cars. A hose connects to the PCV valve, and normally this valve is located in the rocker arm cover, and the other end of the hose connects at the base of the carburetor. To locate the PCV valve on your car engine, refer to your Owner's Manual or ask your mechanic. Some older cars do not have a PCV valve. My Owner's Manual recommends that this valve be inspected at each oil change and replaced every twenty-four months or 24,000 miles, whichever occurs first.

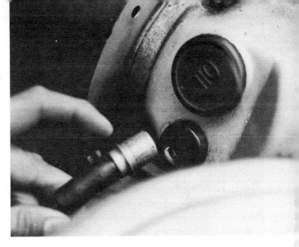

PCV valve

After you locate the PCV valve, remove it from the engine, using pliers to disconnect it from the hose. Shake the PCV valve: if it rattles, the valve is not jammed and is satisfactory; if it does not rattle, replace it. Another way to check it is to crank the engine and put your finger over the end of the PCV valve: if you feel a vacuum, it is all right; if not, it needs replacing.

CHANGING DRIVE BELTS

Things you will need:

    a. New belt(s)—be certain to get the proper type and length
    b. Tools: box wrenches, socket wrenches, etc.
    c. Jack handle

Belts should be changed whenever they show signs of wear, such as frayed edges. It is a good idea to replace all belts every two years or 24,000 miles. Be sure to check the belts if you are starting on a long trip. Modern automobile engines have one or more drive belts; the number of them depends on the accessories you have, such as air conditioning and power steering. In order to change one belt that is frayed or broken, you may have to remove one or more other belts.

Use your box wrenches, socket wrenches, or other tools to loosen or remove brackets and parts obstructing the removal of old belts and the installation of new belts. Most auto parts dealers have belts that will fit both American and foreign cars. Try your foreign car dealer if you cannot find the needed belt for your foreign car at an auto parts store.

Installing a belt with jack handle for leverage

It is important to install the new belt with the proper amount of tension. Use your jack handle to provide leverage on the various pulleys until you have the correct tension in the belt. Then tighten nuts or bolts to keep the tension. The belt tension is about right when you push on the center of a belt between two pulleys 12 inches apart, and the pressure depresses the belt about ¼ to ½ inch. A belt is slipping and should be tightened if you hear a squealing noise when the engine is running. Belt dressing preparation is also available if a belt with proper tension is slipping.

After replacing a worn belt that is not broken, keep the old belt in the trunk of your car as a spare.

19

Hints for Cold Climates

Drivers in northern states where temperatures frequently go as low as 0°F. or colder have special problems. This chapter will help those drivers recognize and overcome the problems. Car care in cold weather is especially important. Check to see that the heater-defroster, windshield sprayer, and windshield wipers are working before cold weather starts. Put a concentrated preparation of antifreeze solution or a deicer in the windshield washer container.

COOLING SYSTEM

Keep permanent antifreeze (ethylene glycol base) in your cooling system in sufficient concentration to protect your engine at the lowest temperature expected locally. The term "permanent antifreeze" means only that the solution will not boil away at normal engine temperatures; it will lose its usefulness eventually. A service station attendant can use a hydrometer to determine the level of concentration in your car. If your cooling system needs more protection, drain one or more gallons of coolant from your radiator and add antifreeze as needed. Refer to your Owner's Manual. Some manufacturers recommend a fifty-fifty mixture of antifreeze and water for year-round operation.

Flush out the cooling system and change the antifreeze every two years. The best water to use with antifreeze for coolant is either distilled water or rainwater. Most ground water contains minerals that form scale in the engine, as does artificially softened water.

The two hoses from the engine to the radiator should be changed when they get soft, usually about every two years; do not wait until a hose bursts. Watch for any leaks in the cooling system. A milky appearance in the engine oil may indicate that antifreeze is leaking internally. Such a problem is serious and requires a mechanic.

Be conscious of whether the thermostat is working properly. The heater should put out heat within two miles or five minutes. If not, the thermostat is defective and should be replaced.

OIL

Refer to your Owner's Manual, and put oil in your engine that is recommended for cold weather. My Owner's Manual lists 5W-30, 10W-30, or 10W-40 oil for temperatures down to zero, and 5W-20 or 5W-30 for temperatures below zero. My manual also states that 5W-20 oil is not recommended for sustained high-speed driving. Always use a well-known brand of oil labeled SE quality.

ELECTRIC HEATING OF THE ENGINE

In areas with extremely cold weather, you can install an electric heating element in the cooling system to warm up the engine on very cold days. This may be a tank heater, a head bolt heater, a block heating element, or something similar. When you buy a new car in a northern state, you can order the car equipped with such a heater from the factory or have the heating unit installed when you buy a car from a dealer. A thermostat in the heating device maintains the proper temperature. The cord from the heater extends near the front of the radiator, so the cord may be plugged into an electric source. Some parking facilities in northern states have a 115-volt outlet so you can plug in your heater cord and keep your engine warm while the car is parked.

You can raise the engine's temperature in another way. Put the car in a garage, place an electric light bulb under the hood, and put blankets or a tarpaulin over the hood. A heated garage is best, but even a garage attached to the house provides your car with a warmer temperature than a garage that is not attached. If you must park outside during very cold weather, park your car with the engine facing away from the wind.

ELECTRICAL SYSTEM

Cold weather puts additional strains on the electrical system, and the system should be checked carefully in the fall. Cold temperatures lower the power output from a battery by reducing the electrochemical reaction rate. At the same time, the power required to crank the engine increases, because cold oil is thicker and has more "drag" than warm oil. Extreme cold may freeze a very weak battery and crack the battery case, so keep the battery well charged. Usually the heater and headlights are used more during the shorter days of winter, reducing the alternator power available to recharge the battery. Replace a weak battery as cold weather approaches. The new battery should be at least as powerful (amp-hour rating) as the manufacturer's recommendation for your car, but a more powerful battery will give an extra reserve of energy.

In extremely cold weather the voltage from the battery to the ignition may be reduced because of the additional amount of power required by the starter. The resulting weaker spark may not ignite the colder fuel-air mixture, and your engine will not start, especially if the ignition system is weak or the engine is poorly tuned. Therefore, have your car tuned before severe weather sets in.

You will be driving more at night and in conditions of poor visibility in winter, so check the lights frequently to make sure all are in good order.

EXHAUST SYSTEM

People spend more time in closed cars in winter. Make sure the exhaust system does not leak carbon monoxide into the passenger compartment. Check the exhaust manifold, muffler, tail pipe, and other parts of the exhaust system for leaks, or have a mechanic do it. Replace any defective part at once.

It is safer to drive with your wing windows open a little, or lower the front windows slightly if you do not have wing windows in your car.

BRAKES

Check the brakes before cold weather to make sure the linings on drum brakes and the pads on disc brakes are in good condition. Replace these components if needed. The brakes should be evenly adjusted. Steering can compensate for uneven braking on dry pavement, but on snow or ice uneven braking is hazardous. The safe way to stop on snow or ice is by using controlled braking, which means that the brake action is directly responsive to your foot pressure—the more you push the more brake action you have. If the brakes grab, they cannot be controlled. Brakes that grab should be overhauled so you will have smooth braking.

TIRES AND CHAINS

Make sure all tires have adequate tread. A bald tire exerts very little side force for turning or skid control. Front tires require good tread for safe steering and stopping. The front wheels transmit about 60 percent of the braking force in normal driving, and you have lost more than half your stopping capability if the tires have little or no tread.

Buy snow tires for the back wheels, or for the front wheels in the case of a front-wheel-drive car. If you buy two extra wheels from a used-parts dealer, you can keep the snow tires mounted and balanced on these wheels. You can keep a snow tire on the spare year around, and then you will only have to buy one extra wheel. You can buy snow tires with studs for use on ice in some states; in other states they are illegal as they can cause road damage.

Two recent technological developments for winter driving are the combination snow-and-ice tire, and the cable chain. The reported advantage of the new tire is that it does not need metal studs, and it is purported to give greater traction and more stopping power than an ordinary snow tire. The cable chain is made from round steel cable. These chains, like the old-style link chains, are designed to turn with the tire and are engineered so that even someone with very little strength can install them on the rear wheels in a few minutes. One big advantage is that the car does not have to be jacked up or the back wheels removed in installing the cable chains. They are designed primarily for emergency conditions—blizzards, crossing a mountain pass

—in which you encounter heavy snow conditions for short periods of time. Cable chains are not designed for extended highway driving or for speeds over 30–35 mph.

Some states require that you use snow tires and carry chains in your car during snowy or icy conditions if you are driving on expressways or mountain roads. Some states require that you use chains under certain extreme conditions.

ADDITIONAL TIPS FOR COLD WEATHER

Keep the fuel tank well filled, especially if your car is stored in a warm garage. Moisture will collect in the fuel tank when you drive the car into a warm area from cold temperatures. An empty tank has more space in which moisture can form. Some experts recommend adding a can of "dry gas" to your gasoline tank every other tank or so, to remove any ice that may form in the tank or fuel line.

Put some liquid graphite in the door locks about every two weeks to prevent moisture from collecting and freezing in zero weather. You can use an electric hair drier with a fan, or a small drier that plugs into the cigarette lighter, to thaw out a frozen lock. Car locks more often freeze when the car is parked outside rather than in a garage. You can also heat your car key with matches or a cigarette lighter and gradually work the key into a frozen lock.

Put a silicone lubricant on the door lining strips every two or three weeks to prevent the strips freezing to the car during wet, cold weather. The silicone lubricant will help keep the doors from freezing shut when the car is washed during freezing weather.

PREPARATION BEFORE DRIVING

Different cars have different cold-starting procedures, primarily based on the carburetor and ignition system designs. Refer to your Owner's Manual, then try minor variations to learn what works best for your car. Different "experts" have different recommendations on "warm-up." Some say a long warm-up, some say a short warm-up, and some say no warm-up. I believe the engine should be warmed up enough to operate reliably and predictably without sputtering, coughing, or stalling when you drive the car.

The heater-defroster and windshield wipers should be in good operating condition and be used as necessary to keep the windshield clean. An ice chopper and scraper with a brush on the opposite end is useful to clean your windows. If the windshield wipers become iced during operation and streak the windshield, stop at the first safe opportunity and clean them; they are not likely to get better by themselves. A cool temperature in the driver/passenger compartment will reduce the tendency of driven snow to turn to heavy slush on the windshield. An antifreeze solution is good for cleaning. If the windows have a tendency to frost over on the inside, you can put acetate frost shields on the inside.

Have an undercoating applied to your car when you buy it to protect against rust from salt that is used on many highways and streets to melt the ice.

EQUIPMENT

Driving your car on ice or snow is different from any other kind of driving, and I advise you to acquire the following equipment. Get a fifty- or one hundred-pound bag of sand to carry in the trunk, and place it equidistant between the rear wheels. The sand will be useful to provide more traction for the rear tires if you get stuck in snow or ice, and the bag's added weight will help the tires grip the road surface better. Or carry a bag of cat litter, which is also very good for providing traction on ice. Two pieces of old carpet, six feet long by one foot wide, are useful to lay on the snow or ice in front of the back wheels when the car is stuck.

Put a shovel in the trunk (it could be a folding trench shovel from an army-navy surplus store) in case you need to dig your way out of ice or a snowdrift. Obtain emergency flares and a twenty-five-foot length of strong nylon rope or ¼-inch steel cable with hooks at each end. The rope or cable is useful for pulling a vehicle out of a snowdrift. In some states the law requires that you carry emergency flares.

DRIVING ON ICE OR SNOW

Remember the limitations of yourself, your car, and the driving surface. You cannot accelerate quickly, turn quickly, or stop quickly on snow or ice. Start gradually by using low gear and accelerating gently. Maximum traction occurs just before the wheels spin; minimum traction occurs while they are spinning. Many cars with automatic transmission have just enough power for the wheels to start the car moving on ice when the accelerator is depressed gently. Pretend there is an egg between your foot and the accelerator. Approach steep downgrades in low gear and stay in low. Go slow! Speeds that are normally safe can be hazardous on ice and snow.

Reaction to a skid should be almost instantaneous, before enough skidding momentum has accumulated to make control impossible. Some drivers react correctly by instinct; others must learn, preferably by practice in safe, controlled situations. An empty parking lot is a good place to practice.

As most skids are caused by the rear of the car swinging around toward the front (rotation), your task is to prevent this. Take your foot off the accelerator and turn the steering wheel to move the front end to the right if the rear end wants to pass on the right. Steer to the left if the rear tries to pass on the left; in other words, turn the wheel in the direction of the skid. If you do not, the rotation will increase until your car spins out of control.

You may encounter the problem of getting out of a snowdrift or off an ice patch. Use the shovel from your trunk to clear a path and the sand, carpet, or cat litter to provide better traction. Put the car in low gear and depress the accelerator gently to avoid spinning the wheels. Drive out slowly. If the car moves forward a short distance and then the wheels begin to spin, try a rocking motion; reverse the car and then come forward, repeating this operation as necessary. Some experts suggest letting some air out of the rear tires to provide more traction. I do not recommend this unless you have a pressurized can or a small electric air pump that plugs into the cigarette lighter to restore the pressure in your tires.

Keep a small hammer under the seat of your car for emergency use. Cases have been reported of drivers on the road for several hours in subfreezing weather who discovered upon stopping that they were imprisoned. The car doors would not open and the windows would not roll down because they were frozen. Use the hammer to break the window glass in case of a severe emergency.

20

Towing a Trailer

Thousands of drivers use their cars or pickup trucks to pull a trailer. The last several years have shown a substantial increase in the purchase and use of recreational vehicles (RV's) and trailers. This chapter can help you if you have to tow any vehicle, whether it is a small boat trailer, a carryall trailer, a tent trailer, or even a large travel trailer.

GENERAL INFORMATION

Refer to your Owner's Manual for information and suggestions before towing any trailer. Passenger cars are designed to be used primarily as passenger conveyances, and a car used for towing a trailer handles differently, requires more frequent servicing, and costs more to operate. Your safety depends on avoiding overloads and using the correct equipment properly. The maximum trailer weight that any car can pull efficiently depends on the weight of the car and the special equipment installed on the car as recommended by the manufacturer. Never tow any trailer unless your car is properly equipped.

The best way to tow a heavy (2,000 pounds or more) trailer and load is with a frame-mounted, load-equalizing hitch that has sway control for stabilization. A hitch that bolts to the frame is better than a welded hitch, because welds sometimes crack or break. Avoid bumper hitches if possible, except on the recommendation of a reputable trailer rental agency. Do not use axle-mounted hitches, which can cause damage to the axle housing, wheel bearings, wheels, and tires. Follow the advice of your trailer dealer or a reputable installer of trailer hitches.

Trailer hitch, showing ball

All trailer hitches should have two safety chains, properly attached. Many states require that the safety chains be attached to the trailer tongue between the ball and the trailer, as the ball is the most likely part to fail in case of an accident.

As a rule of thumb, the tongue load of the trailer should be no more than 10 percent of the loaded trailer weight. Shifting the distribution of the load in the trailer can vary the tongue load. The weight of the tongue load on the rear of your car means you should carry less weight inside your car, particularly in the trunk. Since you need more air pressure in your tires when your car is carrying loads, ask a tire dealer for the correct pressure, but do not put in more than the maximum pounds per square inch (psi) of pressure given on the side of the tire.

Maintenance schedules differ for cars that pull trailers. The automatic transmission should be serviced every 12,000 miles, or twice as often as with normal car use. Change the engine oil about twice as often as you normally do. Depending on the amount of the load to be pulled, the cruising speed, and the distance to be traveled, you may need to install a transmission fluid cooler; consult your automobile dealer.

Mount an ordinary ball-and-socket towing hitch on the passenger side of the front bumper of your car to maneuver a small boat trailer or other small trailers into tight spots. This tip is useful for boat launching or for turning around on narrow roads.

You may be eligible for a trucker's discount on gas if you use a pickup truck to pull your trailer; ask about this discount when you buy gas.

TRAVEL TRAILERS

The following tips will be especially helpful for drivers towing large travel trailers:

Selection of Trailer and Towing Car

Trailers with tandem wheels (four wheels and two axles) have less sway and are more easily controlled on the highway. Do not use small or medium-sized cars to tow medium to large (twenty-two-foot to thirty-foot) travel trailers, or trailers that are too heavy. Check with your car dealer; too big a trailer is unsafe and places a severe strain on the smaller car's body and engine.

You can equip a towing car with a low-ratio differential at the time of purchase or later. It causes the engine to turn faster in relation to the wheels to produce more power, but will also consume more gas when you operate the car without the trailer. An alternative is to select a car with a larger engine and a standard ratio differential.

Some trailer owners use air shocks or booster shocks on the tow car to permit the trailer and car to "level up," which means the shocks on the back of the car can support the weight of the trailer and keep the car level. Booster shocks are especially desirable for a car with soft springs; heavy-duty springs can be stiff and may give you a bumpy ride when you are not pulling the trailer.

Trailer Hitch

Medium to heavy trailers place a heavy load on the rear of a car, and some of this weight must be shifted to the front wheels of the tow car. This weight shift involves tremendous forces in the trailer hitch and at the points where the hitch is attached to the car. Through the use of tension bars, weight-distributing hitches are engineered to distribute hitch weight equally to the four wheels of the tow vehicle and the wheels of the trailer. You should also install one or two sway bars, as they are essential for minimizing the sway of the trailer in poor road conditions, high crosswinds, sudden swerves, and when passing large vehicles, such as trucks.

Buy a hitch that is recommended by a reputable and experienced travel trailer dealer and have the hitch installed by a professional. Examine the hitch often during use, especially during the first few days of towing, paying particular attention to welding that may have developed cracks or other signs of failure. Be certain to install a break-away switch, which usually consists of a cord or fine wire strung between the two halves of the hitch. When the cord or wire is broken for any reason, the trailer's electric brakes are applied automatically. Another system operates when the cord is pulled, closing a switch that activates the brakes. Incidentally, safety chains are required in most states.

Brakes

Heavy trailers cannot be towed safely without the ability to brake the trailer wheels, thus the trailer should have electric brakes. These can be activated manually, or by means of a brake pedal switch, in which case your foot on the brake will operate the electric brakes before the car's brake pedal moves enough to actuate the car's brakes. Test the trailer braking system at the start of each trip after it is hooked up to the car.

Tires

The tow car's tires should be of a high quality, in good condition, and inflated specifically for the load you carry. Radial tires are especially recommended for cars pulling trailers: they are more dependable, give more miles of service, and run cooler under loads than other types of tires. Buy the best tires you can get for your trailer if you are pulling a heavy trailer long distances.

Trailer tires do not give a readily detectable warning when they start going flat. Once flat, the tires are soon ruined if the trailer is moving. Carry a spare wheel and tire for your trailer, and do not forget a lug wrench for your trailer wheels. Every new trailer owner ought to practice changing a tire before he has to do so on the road.

Trailer Jack

Carry a hydraulic jack with ample capacity. With some trailers, if you use a jack under the axle to raise it enough for the bottom of the tire to clear the ground, you will have a hard time getting the spare into the wheel well and onto the hub. A better method is to raise the trailer by placing jack stands under the trailer frame at the front. Then use a hydraulic jack and some wooden blocking under the rear bumper to lift the trailer body up. The axle sags and the tire will go on or come off easily.

Wheel Bearings

Keep an eagle eye on the wheel bearings; be sure they are properly lubricated and adjusted.

Refrigeration

Some types of refrigerators must be level to operate properly. You can use a carpenter's level in the freezer compartment or two small levels that are designed to be mounted on the outside of the trailer.

Cooling

You engine's ability to pull a trailer of a certain weight without overheating depends on several things: the horsepower, the differential gear ratio, the cooling system, the transmission cooling system, the speed traveled, and the terrain. A skillful driver knows the safe range of his car and stays within these limits.

Since your car engine will need to dissipate more heat when you are pulling a trailer, additional cooling capacity is a good investment with heavy trailers. You can order a car from the manufacturer with a "trailer pack," which usually includes a heavy-duty radiator and a transmission fluid cooler; the dealer can install both if the car is not equipped at the factory. Install a water temperature gauge on your car if it has only a warning light to signal heat build-up. Slow down, turn off the air conditioner, or take other steps before the engine gets too hot and is damaged. If you are driving in the mountains, shift to a lower gear before the engine labors and strains.

Insurance

Some states require $100,000/$300,000 minimum liability insurance on all travel trailers. Know your coverage and the insurance laws of your state.

Things You Should Carry for Your Travel Trailer

I recommend that you carry a spare tire and wheel for your travel trailer, a lug wrench for the trailer wheels, and a hydraulic jack of sufficient capacity. Your trailer should have two levels mounted on the outside, one on the tongue end and the other on one side of the trailer. In addition to these, you should carry:

1. Four wheel chocks or blocks
2. Two stabilizer jacks (preferably four)
3. A small shovel
4. An axe
5. A tow rope, about fifty feet of ¾-inch or 1-inch nylon is satisfactory
6. An assortment of small tools, adjustable wrenches, etc.

Confidence

When you first get your travel trailer, practice towing and backing up on a shopping center parking lot, a school ground, or a vacant athletic field. Skillful trailer drivers are not born that way; they achieve handling skills through practice. With a properly equipped car, trailer towing is safe provided the driver is careful and confident.

Parking

You can often find a drive-through pad when parking your travel trailer. When it is necessary to back a trailer into a parking space, you will find it useful to have someone stand outside the car and direct you.

Emergencies

Emergencies and problems may arise when towing a trailer. Keep cool and use common sense, and you can probably solve the problem without undue stress or risk and little or no damage.

If your car brakes fail without warning, activate the electric brakes on the trailer. Apply them firmly with a snubbing action (which means apply brakes, then release, apply, and release). Applying the brakes constantly with no cooling interval may result in the brakes getting so hot they will no longer operate properly. A twenty-foot or larger travel trailer probably has enough braking capability to stop itself and the towing vehicle, if the driver handles the brakes properly. Simultaneously, with automatic transmission, move the gear lever into second gear, then into low. With manual transmission, keep shifting down until the towing vehicle's speed is reduced as much as possible by using the engine as a brake.

What do you do if your brakes fade? The brakes on your car may simply fade away on lengthy downgrades that require frequent braking, a problem that is more likely to occur with drum brakes than with disc brakes. You will smell a strong odor of overheated brake linings. Stop your car and trailer, using the procedure already mentioned. Pull off the road and let the brakes cool for thirty minutes or longer; removing the hub caps will help the hubs to cool quicker. Drive more slowly and in lower gears when you start again, using engine drag for a brake. At the earliest opportunity, get a reputable mechanic to check the condition of your brakes and make any needed repairs.

If you are driving up a steep incline while pulling your trailer, and your engine dies, but the emergency brake will not hold, stop the car with your foot brake, holding it down while you get someone to put wheel chocks or blocks behind the rear wheels of the trailer or the car. If you do not have any blocks of wood, perhaps your helper can locate rocks, logs, bricks, or other material to block the rear wheels. Spare tires and wheels can be used for chocks.

Suppose your trailer disconnects at high speed. When the weight-distributing hitch fails, the trailer tongue will probably sink to the ground, either by breaking the safety chains or by pulling down the rear of the car. Do not slam on the brakes! Doing so will probably snap the safety chain, and the trailer will plow into your vehicle, damaging both of them. Take your foot off the gas and manually apply the trailer brakes. If they are not working, you will have to coast to a stop. Gradually steer to the side of the road. If road conditions permit, drive onto the shoulder to help decrease the speed of the car and the trailer. The breakaway switch should apply the trailer brakes immediately if the trailer breaks away completely.

If you have a blowout at high speed, do not slam on the brakes! Take your foot off the accelerator and manually apply the trailer brakes. Let your car and trailer begin to slow down and get your car's steering under control. Hold the wheel firmly, and gradually edge the car over to the side of the road. Try to avoid using the car brakes, and stop with the trailer brakes instead. If necessary, use the car brakes lightly and cautiously, holding the trailer brakes manually. If there is a wide shoulder, ease the car onto it. If there is no shoulder, use emergency flashers to warn other drivers. It is better to drive on a flat tire to get off a busy highway than to try to change a tire where heavy traffic endangers your life.

21

*Preventive Maintenance
Schedule Summary*

ONCE A WEEK:

Turn on your air conditioner all year round for fifteen minutes a week. Pick a specific time, such as on the way home from church each Sunday or on the way to work each Monday morning, so you will not forget.

EVERY TWO WEEKS OR 500 MILES AND BEFORE TRIPS:

Perform the four regular checks:

1. Engine oil level
2. Liquid level in the battery
3. Air pressure in the tires (observe front tires for wear patterns at the same time)
4. Liquid level in the radiator (water-cooled engines only)

Plan to make these checks at a regular time. Also check for fuel, water, oil, or other fluid leaks by observing the ground beneath the vehicle after it has been parked for a while. Water dripping from the air conditioner after use is normal, but any other leaks may indicate a problem and the source should be located and corrected at once. If you smell gasoline fumes at any time, locate and correct the cause at once because of the danger of fire.

ONCE A MONTH:

Check the liquid level in the windshield washer reservoir.

EVERY 5,000 TO 8,000 MILES:

Rotate tires (see Chapter 11, Tires).

APPROXIMATELY EVERY THREE OR FOUR MONTHS OR 6,000 MILES (follow your Owner's Manual):

Change oil, change oil filter, and lubricate. Check the brake fluid level, the power steering fluid level, and the automatic transmission fluid. Check the PCV valve and the differential.

APPROXIMATELY EVERY TWELVE MONTHS OR 10,000 MILES:

Have a tune-up. Repack the front wheel bearings. Inspect the air cleaner filter element. Have the emergency brake and the brake linings checked.

EVERY FALL IN NORTHERN STATES:

Follow the suggestions given in Chapter 19, Hints for Cold Climates.

EVERY TWO YEARS:

Flush the cooling system and add new antifreeze. Change the two radiator hoses. (See Chapter 18, Tips on Medium Tasks.)

EVERY TWO YEARS OR 24,000 MILES:

Have the automatic transmission serviced. Change the drive belts and replace the PCV valve (see Chapter 18, Tips on Medium Tasks).

As the use of the metric system is gradually increasing in the United States, the appearance of kilometers and other metric measures on both automobile gauges and road signs is cropping up more and more frequently. To help you during this transitional period, here is a brief table that compares miles and kilometers.

MILES PER HOUR COMPARED TO KILOMETERS PER HOUR*

Miles	**Kilometers**	**Miles**	**Kilometers**
10	16	50	80
20	32	55	88
30	48	60	97
40	64	70	113

* One kilometer equals approximately ⅝ mile.

Index

147